Welsh
Pirates

Dafydd Meirion

First impression: 2006
© Dafydd Meirion and Y Lolfa Cyf., 2006

Photo credits: Black Bart's son's Bible by kind permission of Roger
Talbot, Bridgend. Images of Fortunatus Wright's ship and sword
by kind permission of Robin Gore-White, Brynddu.

Cover design: Y Lolfa

ISBN: 0 86243 865 9

Printed on acid-free and partly recycled paper
and published and bound in Wales by
Y Lolfa Cyf., Talybont, Ceredigion SY24 5AP
e-mail ylolfa@ylolfa.com
website www.ylolfa.com
tel (01970) 832 304
fax 832 782

Contents

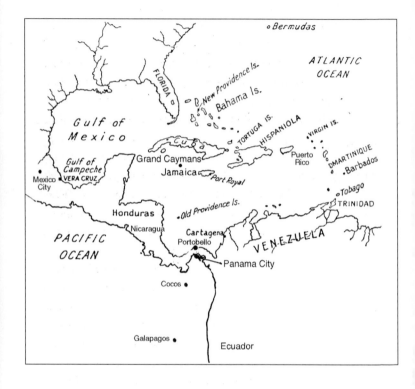

The Caribbean

Introduction

Some sources say that Wales has produced more pirates per mile of coastline than any other country in Europe. Others contend that about half the 17th century pirates were of Welsh descent. This may be stretching it a bit, but, certainly, Welsh pirates such as Henry Morgan and Black Bart were amongst the foremost raiders of the seas during the golden age of piracy. Another source, possibly more reliable, says that 35% of the pirates were English, 20% were whites from the West Indies, 10% were Scots, 8% came from Wales and 2% from Sweden, Holland, France and Spain. It is no surprise, therefore, that there were Welsh pirates on many of the pirate ships, with many of them rising to prominence.

For example, of the crew of twenty-five under English pirate, Captain Edward Lowe, who were hanged, two came from Wales and another had a Welsh name, and of the eight who were found not guilty, one was a Welshman. Of the fifty members of Black Bart's crew who were hanged, five came from Wales and two had Welsh names. Amongst the crew of the Scottish pirate, John Gow, there was one Welshman, one Irishman, a Scot, two Swedes and a Dane.

Who were these pirates? Why did they become raiders of the high seas? Why did piracy come to an end during the 18th century? Did it end? And were the pirates as cruel and drunk as they are portrayed in books and films?

They certainly were drunk and cruel and they attacked merchant ships, with a pistol in one hand and a sword in the other. They were more than enough to scare even the bravest of sailors sailing the high seas. And although we were – and still are – a small nation, Wales has produced more than its share of pirates. There was no one more famous than Captain Henry Morgan, from Rhymney, south Wales; and although most pirates died fighting or on the gallows, Morgan died in bed in Jamaica – mostly from the effects of all the rum that he drank over the years.

Then, there was Black Bart – Bartholomew Roberts, from Pembrokeshire; the first to fly the skull-and-crossbones. He also became one of the most successful of pirates, so successful that the English Navy sent a ship to hunt him down. This they did – off the coast of Africa. He had many Welshmen in his crews, and many of them were hanged on gallows erected on sea cliffs as a warning to others.

Morgan had gone to the Caribbean to seek his fortune, but Roberts was an ordinary seaman – at least in the beginning, until another Welsh pirate captain, Hywel Davis, from Milford Haven, seized his ship. Davis was known as the Cavalier Prince of the Pyrates, and after he was killed in battle, it was Roberts who took over command.

Morgan was a member of the landed gentry, like others who sailed west to seek their fortunes, men like Tomos Prys of Denbighshire and Pyrs Gruffydd from the Penrhyn Estate, near Bangor, who seized numerous Spanish galleons.

But there were also pirates operating nearer home. There are numerous documents from the 15th and 16th centuries that describe Wales as 'a nursery and store-house of pirates'. The islands of Bardsey in the north and Caldey in the south were important centres for pirates attacking ships off the west coast of the British Isles.

The booty would come ashore, not only in isolated creeks, in the depth of night, but also in broad daylight, at some of the main ports, such as Beaumaris, Pwllheli, Cardigan, Haverfordwest and Cardiff. What about the authorities? Weren't they after the pirates? Without the help of the gentry, the pirates would not have lasted long; not only were the most powerful families in the land protecting the pirates, they were also trading with them, and, most often, it was the landowners who got the best bargain – without even getting a foot wet, let alone risking their lives at sea. They were the magistrates, they were the people who had been appointed to keep law and order along the coast – and it was they who had the means and the contacts to enable these stolen goods to be transported to markets as far as Chester, and even London.

Pirates attacked ships unhindered, not only because of the help they received from local landowners, but also because the English Navy was weak. The situation changed after the Spanish Armada, when the navy was strengthened, and piracy along the coast of the British Isles became increasingly difficult. The pirates, therefore, sailed further afield; moving first towards Spain and the Mediterranean, then, towards West Africa, and by the 17th century they had reached the Caribbean.

The early Caribbean pirates were not 'common pirates'. England was at war with Spain, and she had too few ships to guard her coasts and attack Spanish ships further afield. The authorities, therefore, asked the pirates for help, and many a gentleman's son from Wales became captain of a ship that had received permission from the English government to attack Spanish ships sailing from the New World back to the motherland, laden with gold, silver and gems.

There was no need for the English Crown to pay these pirates, or privateers, as they were called. Wasn't there enough booty to be seized from the enemy's ships to make a handsome profit? Many of these privateer captains became very rich – although many lost their fortunes on drink, women and gambling.

The stories of their exploits slowly came back to Wales. Henry Morgan, Black Bart and Hywel Davis became heroes. Stories were told about the romantic adventures of the pirates, in their colourful clothes and gold earrings. Tales were told about maps of remote islands, with crosses denoting where treasure had been buried, of enough cheap rum to sail many a ship, and of the dusky Spanish maidens seized from the enemy's ships and held to ransom.

But life was not always fun. The life of a pirate was a short one. If they weren't killed in battle, they would die of too much rum, of various tropical diseases, or, if they were caught by the authorities, they would swing from the nearest gallows, but, before then, life was grand. With more money in their pockets than their compatriots at home were likely to earn in a lifetime, and cities full of taverns and brothels, even if life was short, it was full of fun.

This is an attempt to collate the adventures of Welsh pirates, off the coast of Wales and on the high seas off Africa and the West Indies, as well as the legends that they left behind here in Wales.

1. Who were the pirates?

What is a pirate?

The legal definition of piracy is 'to seize goods illegally at sea'. The Welsh for pirate is *môr-leidr* (sea-thief) whose meaning is evident, but what about the terms used in English: 'pirate', 'privateer' and 'buccaneer'? What is the difference between these terms, and where did these terms originate?

Before the seventeenth century, there was only one name for these plunderers of the sea and that was 'pyrates' or 'pirates' and *môr-ladron* or *herwlongwyr* in Welsh, although this last term was later used for privateers. One of the earliest recorded uses of *herwlongwyr* comes from the Welsh heroic poems *Brut y Tywysogion*, which mentions that Rhys ap Tewdwr received the help of Irish and Scottish pirates to reclaim Deheubarth in south Wales:

> … *y rodes rys ap tewdwr swllt yr herwlo[n]gwyr*
> *y sgottyeid or gwyddyl adathoed yn borth ydaw.*

The English word comes from the Latin *pirata* and the Latin derives from the Greek *peirates*, from *peirein*, which means to attack. It was during the golden age of piracy, the seventeenth century, when the other terms came to be used.

At times, it was very difficult to differentiate between a pirate and a privateer. A privateer was someone who attacked the enemy's ships – usually Spanish – with the approval of the English Crown, whilst pirates did not have this support. At first, privateers were called private men-of-war. But sometimes it was difficult to say who was a privateer and who was a pirate, with the English Crown changing its allegiances very often; a privateer one day, becoming a pirate the next. For example, Captain Harry Morgan had received the support of the Crown to attack Spanish ships in the Caribbean, but as he fought his way across the Panama isthmus to attack Panama City, England and Spain came to an understanding and, after the attack, Morgan was summoned to London to answer to the charge of piracy, mainly to appease the Spanish ambassador to England.

Privateers would have letters of marque from the Crown; that is a written permission to attack enemy ships. This was an inexpensive method for the English Crown to maintain a navy to attack its enemies in the New World. The captain of the ship was responsible for buying the ship and stocking it, and he and his crew received their 'wage' from the booty. And what if they were caught? Of course, they had acted independently of London, and England was not to blame for these attacks. These letters of marque were published as early as 1295, during the reign of Edward I. It is said that fourteen ships, based in Conwy, had received his permission to attack ships off the coast of north Wales, after the king's ships had been attacked as they supplied his castles along the coast.

What about the term buccaneer? By 1640 the island of Hispaniola (which was ruled then by Spain and is now split into Haiti and the Dominican Republic) was a haven for Caribbean pirates. Wild pigs and cattle roamed the island, after they had been left there by the Spaniards, who soon realised that the island was not a good place on which to rear animals, and that it was much easier to make a living by plundering the natives' gold and silver. Many ex-soldiers reached the island and settled there, and started to hunt the animals that had been left to run wild. The natives' method of preserving meat was to dry it slowly over a fire, to produce *boucan*. The ex-soldiers soon started to use this method, and they became known as buccaneers. At the beginning, these were soldiers rather than sailors, and they preferred to attack towns and cities rather than ships, but, in due course, they became proficient sailors and it became difficult to differentiate between a buccaneer and a pirate.

The age of the Caribbean pirates started in 1571, when Sir Francis Drake (with many Welshmen in his fleet) started to attack Spanish galleons, which were returning to Spain, laden with gold and silver from Mexico and Peru. He had received secret permission from Elizabeth I to attack these ships, and she had made sure that she would receive a share of the booty.

In 1655, Oliver Cromwell sent soldiers (many of them Welshmen who had been captured after fighting in the Royalist armies) to try to capture Hispaniola from the Spanish, but they decided instead to seize Jamaica, and the island soon became the headquarters for British pirates intent on attacking the Spanish fleets.

But it was not only in the Caribbean that pirates operated. Such men had been operating along the coasts of Europe and the Middle East from time immemorial. Most of these pirates received the support of local landowners, some of them very powerful people, with access to the king or queen, and, therefore, the pirates had a free hand to attack ships and towns along the coasts. But during the time of the Spanish Armada, in 1588, Elizabeth I strengthened her navy and life became difficult for the pirates. They soon looked for opportunities further afield, sailing initially to the coasts of West Africa, and later reaching North, Central and South America.

But why did men become pirates?

There were many reasons. One was the poor conditions on the ships of the Royal Navy and English merchant ships. Many had been forced into the navy by press gangs, who roamed the ports looking for young men to press into service. It is recorded that one of the navy's ships, the *Caesar*, was full of men who had been captured in Swansea. The ship was sailing along the south Wales coast when it hit the rocks on Graves End, on the Gower Peninsula. As the men were kept in chains in the hold of the ship, they could not escape, and everyone drowned. On the same peninsula there is a cave called Bacon Hole, where local men would go to hide from the press gangs, with their wives carrying food to them, until they could safely return to their homes.

The work on the navy and merchant ships was very hard and the food poor. The sailors were whipped for the least misdemeanour. The pay was also very poor. Therefore, there was really not much choice, when pirates attacked their ships and gave them the option of being marooned on an isolated beach, or joining them. Although there were also strict rules on the pirate ships, the food was slightly better, there was plenty to drink (on the navy and merchant ships, only the officers were allowed to drink alcohol), and there was every opportunity to make themselves a substantial sum of money. The conditions on board the navy and merchant ships depended to a great degree on the captain – there were a few good captains, but there were many who were not. On the pirate ships, democracy prevailed, and it was the pirates themselves who chose their captain; and if he did not perform well, they would elect another in his place.

It is said that the first question that the pirates would ask the crew of a captured ship was, 'Had the captain been fair with them?' If he had been a cruel captain, his clothes would be stripped from his back and he would be whipped. This would please the crew and they would usually be more than ready to join the pirates.

Black Bart of Pembrokeshire admitted that it was not 'lack of work or anything like it' that made him decide to become a pirate.

"In an honest service ... there is thin commons [food and drink], low wages and hard labour," he said, "but in a pirate life there is plenty and satiety, pleasure and ease, liberty and power, and who would not balance creditor on this side when all the hazard that is run for it, at worst, is only a fore-look or two at choking [being hanged]. No, a merry life and a short one shall be my motto ..."

One time, Black Bart came across thirteen Englishmen who had been marooned by the French on the island of Dominique. When offered the opportunity to join the pirates, they leapt at the chance.

In Captain John Evans' case, it was lack of work in Jamaica that made him decide to become a pirate; this situation, ironically, arose because all the piracy in the area had affected legitimate trade.

According to William Davis, a member of Black Bart's crew, in his testimony in a court of law, after he had been caught off the coast of Africa, he said he was an ordinary sailor who had been caught by Negroes in Sierra Leone. One day, one of Black Bart's ships dropped anchor in the area, and he was released and forced to join the crew. But according to others, Black Bart would never force anyone to join him, and the court declared Davis guilty and he was hanged near the gates of Cape Coast castle. Of the fifty-two prisoners who were hanged at the same time as Davis, five of them were Welsh, as well as a William Williams from Plymouth and another pirate of the same name who, it is said, was 'speechless at execution' and therefore unable to say from whence he came.

In November 1716, the *Bonetto* was seized between St Thomas and St Croix, in the Caribbean, by the pirates, Palgrave Williams, who was of Welsh descent, and Black Sam Bellamy. One of the passengers, a young lad called John King, had pleaded with his mother to be allowed to join the pirates, but she was against the idea. When he threatened to kill her if she would not allow him, she relented and he jumped on board one of the pirate ships.

Not everyone wanted to become a pirate. Welshman Hywel Davis captured a ship in the Caribbean, and on board was a sailor called Richard Jones. He did not want to join his fellow Welshman, but one of the pirates pulled out his knife and slashed Jones' leg. They tied a rope around him and threw him overboard into the shark-infested seas. Suddenly, piracy was an attractive proposition; but later, when the pirate ships had arrived in the port of São Nicolau, off the West Africa coast, Jones jumped ship. It was not long before he was caught, tied to the mast, and whipped by every member of the crew.

Alcohol was the ruin of many a pirate, including Roger Nottinge of London, who, in the seventeenth century, had gone to Ireland to see his sister. There, he received an invitation to go on board Captain James Harris' ship, but he had had one too many and fell asleep. When he woke up, he was tied up in the cabin and the pirate ship was miles out at sea.

John Mansfield, born in Bristol in 1692/3, admitted to the court that he had become a pirate 'for drink rather than gold'. He had become a member of Black Bart's crew and had been caught by the Royal Navy, when Black Bart had been killed. He was so drunk when he was caught, that he awoke a few hours later with no idea where he was.

It was not only sailors who became pirates. Many men, especially from south-west England, had been persuaded to seek their fortunes in the fishing industry in Newfoundland. It may be gold that had attracted the Spanish to the New World, but it was fish that led the English across the Atlantic. The banks off Newfoundland were heaving with cod, some of them as long as six feet and weighing two hundred pounds. After they were caught, they were brought ashore to be cleaned before being salted and sent to England. Hundreds, if not thousands, of men were employed there, having been attracted by the offer of good wages. But once they arrived, they soon realised that they had been duped. Not only was the work very hard but the wages were poor and their expenses were taken from their wages, leaving them with very little, which was usually spent on alcohol. Their masters refused to carry them back home, and as they had no money, they were stuck in Newfoundland, that is, until the pirates – such as Welshman John Phillips, who himself had managed to escape from one of the Newfoundland camps – arrived and offered the men a chance to join his crew.

What about the image we get of pirates in books and films?

Were they as cruel, drunk and as colourful as they are portrayed? Did they have wooden legs? Did they fly the skull-and-crossbones? What about parrots and pieces of eight?

Cruel

Certainly, there were some very cruel men amongst them, who did not think twice before throwing passengers – men and women – overboard, and it is said that Blackbeard (Edward Teach from Bristol) would cut off women's fingers if they were too slow, in his estimation, in taking off their diamond encrusted rings.

It is said that the crew of the *Iven*, with Welshman John Phillips amongst them, 'forced a women passenger one after another', before breaking her back and throwing her overboard.

Englishman Captain Edward Low is reputed to have been one of the cruellest of the pirates. It is said that he once cut off the lips of one of his victims and cooked them in front of him. And such was the cruelty of Frenchman Monbars that he was called The Exterminator. His party piece was to slit open his victim's stomach, take out his guts and nail one end to the mast, before one of his men placed a lighted torch on his behind, to make him dance around the mast until he fell down dead. Another cruel French pirate was Captain Jean David Nau, or L'Ollonais, as he was called, who once cut out a man's heart and ate it in front of the other captives, to try to persuade them to reveal where their treasure had been hidden.

Whilst attacking towns and cities on the coasts of the Spanish possessions in the Caribbean, whole populations were killed or maimed by pirates and privateers.

Some of the captains were also very cruel with their men, but there is only one record of a pirate having to walk the plank, and he was one of Captain Stede Bonnet's men.

One of the rules to which pirates had to adhere strictly to was not to steal from each other – that is, if the victim was alive. When gunpowder was ignited by mistake on board one of Henry Morgan's ships, the *Oxford*, killing many pirates as well as French prisoners, the pirates that had survived the explosion lost no time in jumping into the water, to cut fingers off the bodies floating in the sea, to get at their rings.

Death was the punishment for serious breaches of discipline, and the worst breach was to hide booty from fellow pirates. If culprits were caught, they were tied to the mast and whipped, or left on a desert island with a bottle of water, a pistol and single bullet; that is 'being marooned', from the Spanish word *cimarron*, meaning 'wild'. Stede Bonnet offered the crew of a ship he had captured the choice of joining him or becoming 'governors of a deserted island'.

Drunk

Yes, drink was an important part of a pirate's life. Rum was strong and cheap, having been distilled from sugar cane, which was plentiful on the Caribbean islands. Nearer home, along the coasts of Britain, wine and brandy were many a pirate's booty, and it was often too much of a temptation to drink it, rather than to take it to port to be sold. It was either drunk on the ships, or in isolated coves, when they rested or hid from the authorities. A Captain Snelgrave said that, after his ship carrying claret and brandy was captured by Hywel Davis, the pirates, after drinking as much as they could, started throwing bucketfuls of the expensive drink over each other, before using what was left to scrub the decks.

Many of the pirates were extremely drunk whilst attacking ships; this made them more fearless and angry, and alcohol also helped to relieve pain if they were injured. Seeing a hundred or more drunken pirates on deck was enough to make many a merchant ship yield before a single shot was fired.

There were many towns dotted along the coasts of the Caribbean islands, with dozens of inns and brothels to serve the pirates. Port Royal in Jamaica had the reputation of being the 'richest and worst town in America'. In 1679, it is said that nearly half the four thousand inhabitants were involved with piracy in some way. At that time, Port Royal and Boston, Massachusetts, were the two main settlements in North America. In Port Royal, grand houses and taverns were intermingled with inns and brothels that were full of 'vile strumpets and common prostitutes'. The most prominent brothel offered the services of over twenty women, both white and black. Mary Carleton, originally from London, was the favourite. She was described as 'cunning, crafty, subtle and hot and as common as a barber's chair; no sooner was one man out but another was in'. In Port Royal in 1669, it is said that there was a drinking establishment for every two men on the island.

It is said that, in 1668, a Welshman, Captain John Morris, gave a prostitute in one of Jamaica's brothels five hundred pieces of eight – his entire booty after a raid on Cuba – to take off her clothes in front of his men. He could have had a white prostitute for himself for only fifty pieces of eight, or twenty for a black one.

It is certainly true that alcohol played a great part in pirates' lives – except for a few. Black Bart, although one of the foremost pirates of his day, was a religious man. He held services on a Sunday, and his favourite drink was tea. He also refused to attack ships on a Sunday.

Colourful

Not only were pirates colourful characters, but they also wore colourful clothes. Possibly it is Black Bart who was the characteristic pirate, who gave us the image with which we are familiar today. According to a description of him, he was 'a tall, dark man, he used to wear a rich damask waistcoat and breeches, and a red feather in his cap. Round his neck was a gold chain with a large diamond cross dangling from it; he held a sword in his hand, and two pairs of pistols, hung at the end of a silk sling flung over his shoulders'. And, because of his red waistcoat, the French merchants started calling him *le jolie rouge* (pretty red) and that is the origin of the term Jolly Roger, used for the pirates' skull-and-crossbones flag.

It is said that Henry Morgan would cut his hair short so that he could wear wigs during official functions, but during battle, he would tie a red scarf around his head. He would also wear a hat with a large feather in it; and, usually, a shirt decorated with gold, linen pantaloons, colourful socks, and shoes instead of boots. He had a silk embroidered coat but he would rarely wear it, as it was too hot.

Many of the crew also tied scarves around their heads, to keep their long hair out of the way, when they were fighting or carrying out their duties on board the ships and on shore. Since much of the booty was gems and gold objects, many of them wore gold rings in their ears, or gold chains around their necks. Blackbeard had a dark beard 'up to his eyes', in which he had plaited colourful pieces of ribbon. He also tied small packets of saltpetre to his hat before he attacked ships, and these were fired to give out smoke around his head, to frighten the enemy. The pirates had at least two pistols each, to give them a second chance in case the powder was wet in one of them.

Dangerous

Certainly, the life of a pirate was dangerous, and many lost their hands, arms or legs, and even their lives, during battles. If they survived, some pirate ships had surgeons on board, who would tend to them, such as Welshman Samuel Hopkins, the apothecary. If they lost a hand they would get an iron hook to replace it, and if a leg was cut off – by the enemy or the surgeon – then they would be given a wooden stump instead. If there was no doctor on board, the ship's carpenter would saw off the limb with his sharpest saw. The wound would then be seared, using the mate's axe, which had been placed in a fire until it was red hot, and wounds would be stitched up by the sail-maker.

One who had a wooden leg was Captain François Le Clerc, known as *Jambe de Bois*, or 'wooden leg' in French. 'Compensation' for loss of limbs was paid according to the Ship's Articles. If a pirate lost a hand he would receive six hundred pieces of eight; for losing a leg, five hundred pieces of eight (there was no value on left hands and legs); and a hundred pieces of eight were given if they lost an eye or a finger. If these injuries were caused by fighting amongst themselves, no compensation was given.

Unlike what we see in films, where there are duels using thin rapiers, fighting between pirates and the sailors defending the merchants ships were bloody affairs, the men using heavy cutlasses and axes, which not only caused terrible wounds but also broke bones. Not all attacks led to fighting. When they approached a merchant ship, the pirates would fire one of their cannons as a warning, and if the ship did not stop, they would chase the merchantman and board her. Often, this was unnecessary as the pirates' reputation was enough. Usually, there were not more than a couple of cannon on pirate ships. To carry more would make their vessels too heavy and slow to catch the merchant ships, or to escape from the navy. There was also little point in destroying a ship with cannon fire, as it would then be of no value to the pirates. They would, therefore, fire their muskets before boarding a ship, and since the buccaneers were good shots, after years of hunting, they could kill many of the defenders before going too near. Once they had boarded a ship, they would use their pistols, swords and knives.

Such were the dangers, between the fighting and the drinking and the various diseases, as well as the gallows, it is said that the life of a pirate was only about three years. It is also said that only about a third of the pirates returned home, and Henry Morgan was an exception, having lived to be a comparatively old man, dying in his bed and having kept a lot of his wealth.

Since it was in the tropics that most of the seventeenth and eighteenth century pirates operated, it was natural for them to keep some of the exotic animals that they came across, such as parrots and monkeys. There are numerous records of parrots speaking English, Dutch, French and Spanish, but no Welsh, but with Wales having produced so many pirates, it would be surprising if there wasn't a Welsh speaking parrot somewhere.

The flag and pieces of eight

In the beginning, the pirates flew a plain red (representing blood) or black flag. Black Bart was the first to fly a black flag with a skeleton on it. But rather than a skull-and-crossbones, Black Bart had a skeleton, two skulls and letters of the alphabet (referred to later). In Wales there are numerous gravestones with a skull and crossbones on them (one in Edern, on Llŷn peninsula, and another

Llanfaglan Church

A gravestone at Edern Cemetery inscribed with a skull and crossbones

in Llanfaglan, near Caernarfon), and many believe that they are the graves of pirates, but it was a feature on eighteenth century gravestones with no connection with pirates (but see the story on a later page). It is said that Captain Richard Worley, who was hanged in 1719, was the first to use the skull-and-crossbones we usually associate with pirates.

And what were pieces of eight? These were Spanish coins – *pesos* – about the same size as our fifty pence pieces, with a Spanish coat of arms on one side and the figure eight on the other, representing eight *reals*, which was a Caribbean currency. These coins were made of silver that was mined and minted in Central America and shipped by the millions to Spain – unless the pirates got them first.

It is said that Henry Morgan stole a million pieces of eight (worth about £50 million in today's money) and Black Bart acquired the same amount in gold and silver.

But what evidence is there that pirates stole these fabulous amounts? There are numerous records of what the pirates stole from merchant ships, and, fairly recently, divers found the wreck of the *Whydah*, one of pirate Black Sam Bellamy's ships, on the sea bed near Cape Cod, in North America. So far, over eight thousand pieces of eight, seventeen gold bars and fourteen pieces of gold, as well as gems have been found – and they've only started on the work of recovering the treasure. But it wasn't only by stealing it from ships and coastal towns that pirates got their gold and silver. There are numerous records of Henry Morgan, Black Bart and others demanding ransom for prisoners, as Morgan did after the raid on Portobello.

There was also another way for the ordinary pirate to make money. The first pirate to see a merchant ship on the horizon would receive the best pair of pistols on the ship, after she had been seized, and these were usually worth about £30.

It was not just gold and silver that they plundered; gems were also a favourite amongst the pirates. Captain John Taylor and his crew stole over a million pounds worth of gems, in today's money, from Lagoa in Lorenzo Marques Bay, in April 1722. The gems were shared: forty-two to each pirate, but one of them received a huge gem, which was worth as much as forty-two gems, but he was not satisfied – he wanted the same as everyone else, so he took a hammer and smashed it to pieces.

Order on board ship

The impression is that pirates were wild, unruly, uncivilised men, but there were many captains of good backgrounds amongst them, such as Henry Morgan and Pyrs Gruffydd. It was necessary to have order on board ship, for it to function properly, and this was achieved by using what was known as the Custom of the Coast, or Ship's Articles. This was a form of early democracy, and every member of the crew had to sign the Ship's Articles before starting on a voyage – swearing an oath on a Bible, and, in the case of Black Bart's crew, on a Welsh Bible. Once the fighting had started, the captain – some of whom had no power at all on land – had the last word. The whole crew would decide which ships to attack, and the Articles would state how the booty would be shared – five shares for the captain, two for the mate and quartermaster, and one for each sailor.

The Articles would also state how justice would be administered. There was an incident when two English pirates, Porter and Tuckerman, had stolen one of Black Bart's ships, after trying to become friendly with him. They had received goods from Black Bart, as he thought that they were about to join him, but they disappeared with the goods. They were caught and dragged before a 'court of law' on board one of the ships. A large bowl of rum punch was placed on a table on the deck, along with clay pipes and tobacco, with representatives of the pirates sitting around the table, as was required by the Articles. The two prisoners were brought up from the hold and the charges were read to them. They were immediately pronounced guilty, but there was a great deal of discussion on what the punishment would be. Although one of the 'judges', a pirate called Valentine Ashplant, argued against executing the two men, they were eventually tied to the mast, and shot by four men who had been chosen by the pirates.

It needed great skill to keep order amongst men such as Black Bart had under his command. There was a great deal of drinking and fighting and, in one incident, whilst in the Caribbean, he had to discipline one of his pirates because he was so drunk. They started arguing, and Black Bart shot the drunkard dead, but a friend – a pirate called Jones – leapt to the dead man's defence. He attacked his captain, but Black Bart ran him through with his sword. Although wounded, Jones threw Black Bart over one of the cannon and started beating him. Some of the pirates leapt to Black Bart's defence, others joined Jones, and there was a free-for-all on the ship's deck – until the quartermaster put a stop to the fighting, as he considered that Jones should not have challenged Black Bart's authority. When Jones' wounds had mended, the pirates voted that he should be whipped twice across his back.

Of course, it is the stories of the Caribbean pirates that we get from books and films that provide us with our impressions of these men, but there is no reason to doubt that, although their dress may not have been as colourful, the marauding pirates who sailed along the coasts of Wales had the same attributes as their counterparts further afield.

How do we know that so many of these pirates were Welsh?

We know about the ancestry of pirates such as Henry Morgan, Pyrs Gruffydd and Tomos Prys. There are numerous references to the fact that Black Bart and Hywel Davis came from Wales. There are also references to other pirates described as 'Welshmen' or 'Welsh pirates'. With some, we have to go by their surnames. Because we go back many centuries, it is reasonable to assume that many of those with surnames such as Williams, Jones and Davies and operating along the coasts of Britain, if not directly from Wales, had a connection with Wales. And there is plenty of evidence that those marauding in the Caribbean seas during the seventeenth and eighteenth centuries, if not born in Wales, were of Welsh descent.

Although many of the pirates were Welsh – and many of them Welsh-speaking, how much Welsh was spoken amongst the pirates? Many would have had very little English, when they first went to sea, but they learnt English very quickly, and possibly other languages, such as Spanish, French or Portuguese. There is very little reference to the Welsh language in various records, but here is one about a Captain Owen, who, in 1540, attacked a Breton ship near the Scilly Isles and threw the crew overboard.

'Captain Owen called to Phillip the Welshman and the other Welshman, speaking in Welsh, and at one or two of the clock in the afternoon the said Phillip called up the Bretons [I wonder if their fellow Celts, the Bretons, understood some Welsh] one after another to the number of seven men and brought every man to the waist of the ship and caused John the mariner of Weymouth to bind their hands on cross behind their backs.'

Since there were so many Welshmen on the ships of Black Bart, Hywel Davis and Henry Morgan, there must have been some Welsh spoken between the captains and their crew.

2. Raiders of the Welsh coast

If you were to travel from Caernarfon towards Porthmadog or Pwllheli and looked to your left, just before reaching a large house that is now owned by the health service, you will see an old wall. This is a Roman wall that at one time ran down from the Roman fort of Segontium to a port on the river Seiont. Ships sailed to this fort from all over the Roman world, bringing goods to the Roman settlement in the area. There were also fast ships based here to guard the cargo ships from attacks, mainly from Ireland, and it is quite possible that these Irish raiders were the first pirates to operate along the shores of Wales.

There is mention of Saint Cybi visiting a synod or convention in Llanddewi Brefi in AD545, where he was asked for advice by a number of priests, who were intending to travel to Bardsey Island and who were afraid of being attacked by Saxon raiders operating in the area. Cybi told them that, if their faith was strong enough, they did not have anything to worry about. We do not know if they arrived safely at their destination.

In 1080, Robert of Rhuddlan built the first Norman castle at Degannwy, but, a few years later, he was killed whilst attacking 'Welsh pirates' off the Great Orme.

We reach the 12th century before piracy is next mentioned in Wales, although Vikings attacked ships and settlements along the Welsh coast up to this period. From the 12th century onwards, the south Wales coast was notorious for piracy, mainly because Bristol, the second busiest port in England after London, was within reach.

There are numerous caves, creeks and islands along the coast, which were used by pirates to hide themselves and to hide their booty.

Mathew Paris, in his *English History from the year 1235 to 1273*, mentions a gang of Welshmen capturing an Irish ship that was carrying food and wine to the English army at Degannwy. There were sixty barrels of wine onboard, and the English did not receive any of them.

During the 17th century, a Captain Mainwaring from Shropshire described Wales as 'a nursery and store-house of pirates' because of the numerous creeks and bays along the coast and the fact that it was easy to escape to the open seas if they were being pursued.

It can be said that the beginning of the 17th century was the golden age of piracy off the coasts of Britain. The early years of the reign of James I was a period of peace and, therefore, the English navy and armies were reduced. In fact, 50,000 men were discharged from the English Navy during this period. This meant two things: there were hundreds, if not thousands, of experienced sailors with not much to do, and there were few warships to guard the merchant ships sailing along the coasts. Therefore, many, with the connivance of the local gentry, turned to piracy to make a living.

South Wales

In 2002, the remains of a 15th century ship were found by workmen digging foundations for an arts centre on the banks of the Usk in Newport. According to the experts, it could have been a Portuguese ship that had been captured by pirates, possibly under the command of the Earl of Warwick (1428–1471), who owned vast tracts of land in Newport. The ship could have been there to be repaired, and there is a record of the Earl paying a bill for repairing a ship, a few months after he took Newport into his possession.

In 1578, one of the English navy's ships, the *Flying Hart*, was sent to south Wales to try to capture pirates who were attacking ships in the Bristol Channel, but the ship itself was attacked by the pirates off Newport. Two centuries earlier, in May 1383, there is a record of a Genoese ship being captured off Tenby, and that the pirates had brought her to the harbour to unload the two barrels of gold and other goods that were on board.

In 1556, after the inhabitants of south Wales had implored Elizabeth I to help them stop attacks by pirates, she issued a proclamation that every pirate caught was to be hanged on cliffs above the sea, as a lesson to other pirates. What effect this had it is difficult to say, but we do know that, in 1618, Mathew Giles, the revenue officer at Aberthaw, was killed by French pirates.

By the middle of the 16th century, Tenby had become a centre for Breton pirates. In the 1530s, fifteen of them, including Captain John du Laerquerec, were caught when they came ashore for supplies, but when the rest of the crew saw what had happened, they sent three boats full of armed men to try to rescue their captain. They failed, and Laerquerec and his men had to stand trial for piracy.

Off the coast of Pembrokeshire, in 1546, the pirate Richard Vaughan captured the Spanish ship *Sancta Maria de Leusa*, and sold her cargo in the county.

In 1555, pirates who had captured a Breton ship, brought her to Tenby, but they were arrested by Sir John Wogan, Sheriff of Pembrokeshire. Rather than return the cargo to its owner, John le Barthicke, Wogan took the goods and sold them. The Breton owner took Wogan to the Privy Council in London, and Wogan had to pay him compensation.

Caldey Island was also a centre for pirates. The Crown Records of 1562 state that pirates received sheep and other goods here, 'sometimes without leave of the owners'. It added that Fishguard was 'a great resort and succour of all pirates ...' It was said that the inhabitants of Caldey used horses, rather than oxen, to till the land, in case pirates stole them to eat.

Things were also as bad along the south Wales coast during the 17th century, and a prominent local sailor, Sir Thomas Button of Dyffryn, near St Nicholas, was appointed Admiral of the King's Navy on the seas between Wales and Ireland. He had three ships under his command, and he spent a number of years chasing pirates – sometimes successfully, sometimes not. During this period, pirates from France, Spain and Turkey attacked ships sailing along the south Wales coast, and one of their favourite spots to seek shelter was off the Penarth headland.

Pirates not only attacked ships, they also attacked some of the ports along the coast. In one instance, pirates threatened to attack Fishguard. In 1779, the crew of the American privateer, *Black Prince*, captured a local ship outside the harbour and threatened to fire on the town if the inhabitants did not pay a ransom of £1,000. They refused, and the pirates fired their cannon towards the town, hitting a number of buildings. The marks that the shot left could be seen on the wall of one hotel until the 20th century. In the harbour, there was an armed ship that was used by smugglers, and its crew fired on the pirate ship, forcing it to leave the area. After this incident, eight cannons were placed in the fort that protected the harbour.

North Wales

It was not only in south Wales where piracy was out of control. There were numerous islands, coves and harbours along the north Wales coast that were frequented by pirates. Among these was Bardsey Island, owned by local squire, Sir John Wyn of Bodfel, with its old abbey used to store stolen goods and supplies for the pirates. John Wyn had a network of people who would distribute the stolen goods throughout north Wales, and he would also sell supplies such as food, drink and ropes to the pirates. It is said that John Wyn and his men were 'at all times ready to deliver to all such pirates ... victuals and necessaries, when and as often as they have need, receiving again of them for the same large recompense as wine, iron, salt, spices ...'

The privateer, Tomos Prys, would frequently use the island as his hideaway, according to tradition, building a house for himself there.

The nearby St Tudwal Islands were also used by pirates. In September 1563, a pirate called Captain Sergeant came to the islands, with two ships full of grain that he had recently captured. A certain John Roberts of Caernarfon bought the cargoes, but soon afterwards, a local man, John Griffiths, with eight of his men, seized the grain in the name of the Queen.

In St Mary's Church, Conwy, there is a marble plaque to pirate Nicholas Hookes, the son of a local merchant, who frequently visited Bardsey and St Tudwal islands. It is said that he had twenty-seven children and that he was the 41st child of his parents. He died in 1637.

In 1602–3, the inhabitants of Pwllheli were accused of helping pirates, who were led by Sir John Wyn of Bodfel; they had refused to testify against the pirates. They were accused of helping the pirates 'at all times', according to the Star Chamber records, and, in 1626, a number of inhabitants were charged with selling butter and cheese to pirates from Dunkirk, who had called for supplies at the harbour.

The Admiralty was notified in 1631 that a 600-ton pirate ship under the command of John Norman, full of wines and linen, had arrived at Pwllheli. Some of the pirates were captured and imprisoned, but the rest of them escaped by seizing a 300-ton merchant ship, carrying 26 guns, and sailing out to the open sea. Vice-Admiral Griffiths of Madryn tried to go after the pirates to arrest them, but the inhabitants of Pwllheli refused to help him. In 1633, the pirates returned in the ship that they had stolen and attacked a Scottish ship in the harbour. The magistrates tried to capture them, but the locals had warned the pirates and they once again escaped. It is said that a Bristol merchant, who was in the town on business, helped the captain of the pirates to escape, by lending him his horse.

Early in the 17th century, between 1600 and 1610, a chain of stone watchtowers was built along the north Wales coast by Sir

The monastery on Bardsey Island

Thomas Mostyn and his son, Sir Roger Mostyn, both being sheriffs of the counties of Caernarfon, Anglesey, Denbigh and Flint. As they were the largest landowners between the Conwy and Dee rivers, it was their responsibility to guard the coast and ships from pirates. Many pirates from the Isle of Man and Ireland, and as afar away as North Africa, regularly attacked the coast. Four towers were built, each one with an iron basket with a fire in it, at Bryniau, between Degannwy and Llandudno; on the top of the Parish Church of Llandrillo, Rhos-on-sea; on a hill behind Abergele; and in Whitford, Flintshire – covering an area of about twenty-five miles. It is also recorded that similar towers were built by other landlords along the coasts of Anglesey and Llŷn. When a suspected pirate ship was spotted on the horizon, the fires in the iron cages were lit, giving out thick smoke during the day and flames during the night, to warn the inhabitants. Each tower could be seen from the next one to it. This was a very efficient means of warning people, as the warning could travel much faster than the pirate ships.

It was not just goods that the pirates were after. Around 1625, North African pirates attacked Holyhead and seized a hundred people for the white slave market. At around the same time, Moorish pirates pillaged Lundy Island, in the Bristol Channel, over a period of a fortnight, before seizing all the inhabitants and carrying them away. The men were sold as oarsmen in Arab galleons, whilst the women were sold as maids and prostitutes. The tongues of many of them were cut out before they were sold. However, it was not only people who were seized in Holyhead; it was an important port for traffic to Ireland, and the mail service was often targeted by pirates. In 1656, pirates attacked two ships carrying the mail to Ireland. The two captains were sent ashore with a message from the pirates, demanding £80 to release the ships and their cargoes

St Trillo Church tower where a fire was lit at one time to warn of pirates

– and the authorities had no option but to meet their demands.

Because of the problem with pirates, the tower of St Cybi's Church in Holyhead was raised seventeen feet, to enable it to be used as a watchtower, to look out for pirates.

By the end of the 17th century, Britain was at war with France, and the ships sailing from Holyhead were targets for French privateers. In 1680, the ferry *Grace* was seized in Dublin Bay by two French privateers, who demanded a ransom of fifty guineas for it. After they had paid the ransom, when the ship was returned, its owners found that the privateers had taken everything of value from it. By 1693, there were eleven French privateers operating between Holyhead and Chester, and the Royal Navy sent armed ships to guard the merchant ships plying their trade along the coast, but they were not always successful, for, in 1696, four ships bound for Dublin – three from Liverpool carrying salt, and one from Mostyn with a cargo of coal – were seized near Holyhead by French pirates. A ransom was paid and they were released, but they were seized again by another pirate, before they reached Dublin.

In 1710, a French ship, waving the Union Flag, approached Holyhead. It fired one of its guns, but Maurice Owen, the local revenue collector, thought that it was signalling that it was in distress. He rowed out to the ship and was welcomed aboard. He was questioned about the port's defences by the officers, whose intention was to attack it. Owen was locked in one of the cabins, but before the privateers could attack Holyhead, a storm brewed up and the ship was blown towards the shore. The crew tried to lighten the ship, to make it more manoeuvrable, by throwing fourteen of their cannon overboard, and they fired the others to try to summon help. The people on the shore were too frightened to go out to help them, and, eventually, the ship was driven onto the shore at Penrhos, a few miles east of Holyhead. The following morning, after the storm had subsided, seven armed boats left Holyhead for Penrhos, capturing a hundred and fifty French privateers and rescuing Maurice Owen. The privateers were later imprisoned in Dublin.

But it was not only French ships that were causing trouble along the north Anglesey coast. By 1780, the American privateer *Black Prince* was in the area. She seized two of Holyhead's six ferries: the *Beesborough* and the *Hillsborough*. The Americans demanded a ransom, and this, plus the expense of re-equipping the ships, cost the General Post Office a total of £1,067.

Amongst the pirates that ravaged the Welsh coast were:

Marisco or William Marsh (1235? – 1242)

He was one of the pirates that used Lundy as his headquarters. Marisco was the son of an Irish chieftain and was known as the Night Hawk of the Bristol Channel. He would attack ships sailing between the Mull of Galloway and Land's End, mainly seizing people, whom he kept in dungeons on Lundy until ransom was paid by their relatives. It is also said that he traded with the monks of Margam Abbey. Marisco and his men were caught by the king's soldiers, on Lundy in July 1242, and hanged. The present day inn on Lundy is called Marisco's Tavern.

Colyn Dolphin (died 1470)

He was a prominent 15th century Breton pirate, who used the islands of Sully and Lundy to shelter. One of his greatest exploits was the capture of Sir Harry Stradling of Saint Donat's Castle, as he was crossing from Somerset to south Wales. Stradling had to pay the pirate a ransom of 2,200 marks before he was released, and he had to sell most of his estates to find this amount, but Stradling was determined to get his revenge on Dolphin. It is said that he built a tower and placed a light on it to lure Dolphyn's ship onto the rocks. The pirate ship was destroyed on Nash Sands, and Dolphyn was either buried up to his neck in sands near Tresilian, by Stradling's men and drowned when the tide came in, or he was hanged and buried in the sands near St Donat's Castle.

John Callis, Callys or Callice (late 1550s – 1586)

By the 16th century, the number of pirates operating off the south Wales coast had increased dramatically, mainly due to the fact that many of the landowners and naval officers supported them.

One of these was John Callis, who had been born in Tintern, Monmouthshire. He was related to the Earl of Pembroke and the Herberts, and had received a good education. He was later sent to London, to be apprenticed to a haberdasher. Some say that he was pressed into the navy in 1571, but certainly, by 1574, he was being accused of being a pirate and captain of a ship called *The Cost Me*

Noughte. He used his links with the powerful families of south Wales to attack ships in the area without hindrance, and they would also buy the goods that he had stolen. He was friendly with the head of the navy in Cardiff, staying in his house when he came ashore. He would also stay with William Herbert and Sir John Perrot's agent in Haverfordwest. He was described by the Admiralty as 'a notorious pyrate haunting the coasts of Wales', and was known to be the leader of a gang of pirates that operated off the south Wales coast.

John Callis was the most prominent pirate attacking ships off the south Wales coast and Bristol Channel, but he also operated as far as Cornwall and France, and even ventured as far as Denmark and the Azores. By this time, he was described by the Privy Council as 'the most dangerous pyrate in the realm,' and he had a number of ships under his command as well as crews from as far away as the Netherlands and Portugal.

One of Callis' most important customers was Sir John Wogan, an officer in the navy, who, it is said, would sell guns to local pirates. Callis also traded with the Glamorgan Sheriff, Nicholas Herbert, former mayor of Cardiff, William Herbert, Edward Cemais of Cefn Mabli, and John Thomas Fleming of Treffleming. He was also on friendly terms with Thomas Lewis of the Van, Caerphilly, and is said to have used his friend's house to store his goods. Callis would visit many of the mansions of Glamorgan and the inns of Cardiff and Penarth, to sell his booty.

In 1574, Callis seized an Italian ship, *Grace of God,* and sold her cargo in Cardiff and Bristol, and in December of that year, he was in the Azores, where he attacked a Portuguese ship that was carrying sugar and timber from America. But, on the 15th May 1577, Callis was caught on the Isle of Wight and transported to London, where he was kept in the Tower. He was later moved to Winchelsea, where he was interrogated by the Judge of the Admiralty, Dr Lewis of Abergavenny. Callis was accused of ten counts of major piracy and numerous other instances of minor piracy. He was found guilty and sentenced to death, but, in order to save his skin, he decided to help the authorities rid the British coasts of pirates, by telling who amongst the landed gentry were supporting them. Amongst the large landowners that were named by Callis was Nicholas Herbert, who was not only the Sheriff of Glamorgan, but also Callis' father-in-law. The head of the secret service, Lord Walsingham, arranged for Callis to be released on a technical matter.

In July 1578, Callis was free, but it was not long before he returned to his old trade. He received a French ship that had been captured by Sir Walter Raleigh; he returned her to her owners but kept the cargo, and, in 1579, the Admiralty forced him to pay £4,000 (about £4 million in today's money) to the Frenchmen. He refused, but later he did pay £505 to the owners of a Danish ship, which he had seized.

In 1578, Callis brought to Cardiff a Spanish ship, *Our Lady of Conception*, which was carrying wool to Bruges merchants. The owner of the ship complained to the Admiralty, and two men who had bought some of the wool from Callis, William Herbert and Robert ap Ifan, were ordered to pay him compensation, but they refused. Callis had taken the rest of the cargo to Denbigh to be sold. After this incident, a number of the Cardiff and Glamorgan gentry, including the Sheriff, were called to London, to explain why they had not arrested Callis.

In 1582, an old friend of Callis, William Fenner, was commissioned to capture Spanish and Portuguese pirates, and he appointed Callis as his lieutenant. It was not very long before he had captured a number of ships – in fact, many of these were neither

Spanish nor Portuguese. In March 1583, he seized two Scottish ships and sold their cargoes in Plymouth. On board one of these ships were religious books on their way to James VI. Callis sold them to a Huguenot printer for £40. A year later, he captured a French warship; he was made captain of the ship and he used her to attack French and Portuguese ships. Sometime in the 1580s, he was arrested in Ireland, but he escaped and later attacked a number of French ships.

The authorities were after him now, mainly because of the £4,000 he owed to the French ship-owners. He found it difficult to operate along the coasts of Britain, and he was forced to sail towards North Africa, and it is there – in either 1596 or 1587 – that he was killed. But one source (Captain John Smith of Pocahontas fame)

Old Point House in Angle, Pembrokeshire

says that he was hanged in Wapping, with two other pirates who used to raid the Welsh coast.

When he raided along the Welsh coast, Callis would frequently call at the Old Point House in Angle, Pembrokeshire. The inn is still there, with the fire in one of the bars having been kept going over the centuries, until a few years ago, when the owners were advised to extinguish it because of safety fears.

Thomas Carter

In June, 1535, Carter attacked a Breton ship, carrying salt and wine, off the coast of Pembrokeshire. After selling the goods to the local gentry, who included the Bishop of St David's, he sailed the ship up to north Wales. There, he was caught by Sir Richard Bulkeley of Beaumaris and taken to London to be hanged. His crew were imprisoned in Caernarfon Castle, but five of them managed to escape.

Captain John Paul Jones

It is said that John Paul Jones, who took a leading part in the American War of Independence, visited the island of Caldey several times, and some say that he was buried there. Jones was born in Scotland around 1728, the son of one of Lord Selkirk's gardeners. He went to sea when he was twelve years old, but returned later to Scotland and joined a band of smugglers. After he had saved enough money, he bought a ship, became a pirate and raided the English coast. It is said that he visited Caldey to get fresh water and supplies, and one of the bays of the island is named after him. He is also said to have visited Fishguard and fired on the town, to try to force the inhabitants to pay ransom for a merchant ship that he had captured. He is also mentioned in the Plas Newydd (Anglesey) papers, as having raided off the north Wales coast.

But the authorities were soon after him and he escaped to the Caribbean. When the American War of Independence started, he was given his own ship and he used her to attack English ships, from 1777 onwards. He later returned to Scotland, to try to capture Lord Selkirk, but he failed. In a fierce battle with English warships off the coast of Scarborough, he was forced to surrender. Some say he died in Paris in 1792, others say that his body was pushed into a crevice in the rocks off Ord Point in Caldey.

Even today, there are stories that the ghosts of John Paul Jones and his men are to be heard every now and then on Caldey, burying their treasure – the sound of spades on the pebbles on the beach.

3. The support of the gentry

To steal goods from ships is one thing, but what to do with them afterwards could have been a problem, but the pirates operating off the Welsh coasts could rely on the support of the landed gentry, who not only had contacts throughout Wales and England, but were also those responsible for law and order. It was usual for the pirates to keep about twenty per cent of the money that they received from the sale of the stolen goods; the rest would be shared between a number of 'receivers', these being the local landowners and their agents, and with the support of these powerful people, it was very difficult for the authorities to catch the pirates. Amongst the great families of north Wales that traded with the pirates were the Bulkleys of Anglesey, and the Griffiths family of Cefnamwlch, Llŷn.

Bardsey Island

In the Calendar of Wynn Papers, Bardsey is described as 'a very convenient place for pirates'. During the 16th century, pirates George Morgan and Nicholas Hookes, and local landowners used the islands of Bardsey and Tudwal as their headquarters. One of these landowners was John Wyn ap Huw, of Bodfel, near Pwllheli (d. 1576), who was described as 'chief captain of the pirates of Ynys Enlli [Bardsey]', in a complaint made to the Star Chamber in 1569. He had fought with the Duke of Northumberland's forces in 1549, and had received Bardsey as a reward for his efforts. The island became a centre for pirates to relax after weeks at sea, and a place where they could buy food and drink and ship's supplies such as ropes, ready for their next raids. It was also used to store their stolen goods. John Bodfel and his network would sell these goods in markets and fairs in places as far away as Chester, and because of his good connections with those in authority, he could ensure that the pirates would not be apprehended. But pirates were not always successful in hanging onto their booty.

When Captain Thomas Wolfall brought a shipload of grain, which he had seized in the English Channel, to Llŷn in 1563, John Bodfel boarded her and helped the captain to sell the cargo, as he could not speak Welsh. And when searchers came on board, to try to seize the grain, John Bodfel and another landowner, William Glynne, sent them away, saying that they had more authority than the searchers. One of the Griffiths of Cefnamwlch also went on board to try to claim the grain, but Wolfall said that he had a letter from the Earl of Warwick, giving him permission to attack foreign ships. When John Griffiths asked to see the letter, Wolfall told him that there was no point as the letter was in French. Griffiths then said he would take it a local squire, who could read that language, but, somehow, Wolfall could not find the letter.

John Griffiths appealed to the authorities for permission to seize the grain, but he was refused. Griffiths' next move was to plot with a Bristol merchant called John Thorne, who was staying at his house, to come with him, on the pretext of buying the cargo, but they went with thirty armed men, took the grain from Wolfall, and sold it openly in Barmouth.

In 1567, Morgan ab Ieuan accused John Bodfel of using Bardsey for piracy, and he started a case against him in the Star Chamber, but nothing came of it. John Bodfel faced a similar charge again in 1569, but, again, Bodfel remained free and carried on trading

Beaumaris harbour

with the pirates.

Piracy carried on into the 17th century in the area, and it is said that, in 1659, Bardsey pirates captured a total of twelve ships.

Beaumaris

During the 16th century, Sir Richard Bulkeley, the Vice-Admiral of Anglesey, ruled large areas of Anglesey and Caernarfonshire. Haynes, the pirate, would bring his booty to the port of Beaumaris to be sold, and it is said that he walked the streets of the town without any hindrance. One of Sir Richard's brothers was a solicitor in London, and it is said that he had invited one of the capital's grocers to Sir Richard's house there, to examine casks and chests of sugar that had been transported from Beaumaris. He bought them for £122. In the Admiralty records a mention is made of a pirate called Ffetiplace having landed "dusky sugar ... wines, molasses and Castille soap" at the port of Beaumaris.

One of the Earl of Leicester's agents complained to the Star Chamber that Sir Richard was encouraging his two brothers, Charles and David, to take part in acts of piracy, and that he allowed the port of Beaumaris to be used by pirates. His brother-in-law, Griffith John Griffiths of Cefnamwlch, was also accused of helping pirates, and his son was one of the pirates that used Beaumaris to bring his booty ashore. It is said that he hid a lot of his stolen goods in various properties in the town. One time, the Admiralty seized Griffiths' son's ship, but Sir Richard bought the ship for a paltry sum.

Cardiff

This was another centre for piracy, where the pirates sold their booty to local merchants, mainly due to the fact that much of Glamorgan and the south-east was ruled by the powerful Herbert family.

John Callis would visit the mansions of Glamorgan and the taverns of Cardiff and Penarth, to sell his booty. Amongst his customers were the Sheriff of Glamorgan, Nicholas Herbert, the former mayor of Cardiff, William Herbert, Edwards Cemais of Cefn Mabli, and John Thomas of Treffleming. It was the Herbert family that was in charge of the port of Cardiff; and the head of customs and the Admiralty's representative in Cardiff were Herbert men.

John Callis would stay with Nicholas Herbert, his father-in-law, when he was in Cardiff. Callis was also on friendly terms with the head of the navy in Cardiff, and stayed with him on numerous occasions. He would also stay in Cardiff with William Herbert, and with Sir John Perrot's agent in Haverfordwest.

In 1576, the Admiralty sent a commissioner called John Croft to

Cardiff, to try to discover why Callis was allowed to sell his goods in the area, but he received no help from the inhabitants. During the same year, Callis seized a ship carrying fish from Newfoundland and brought her to Cardiff, after imprisoning the crew in the hold. The Vice-Admiral of Monmouth, Sir William Morgan, sent his men to buy the cargo, and the ship was sailed to Newport, but Croft was after them. Morgan's men were unloading the ship, whilst the men in the hold were shouting for food and drink. Croft appealed to two local magistrates, William Morgan of Llantarnam and Rowland Morgan of Machen, for help, but they refused. Both were members of the powerful Morgan family who were related through marriage to the Herberts. William Morgan was also one of the Vice-Admirals of Wales, the governor of Dungarvan and a Marshal in Ireland.

Dr David Lewis of Abergavenny, a judge in the Admiralty High Court in London, said that influential men in Wales would not arrest John Callis; otherwise, they would lose the source of their wealth, and that they would only pretend to make an effort to catch him.

But it was not only the gentry of south-east Wales that would take advantage of Callis' trade. The Clerk to the Council of Wales and the Marches would send his men to Cardiff, to buy salt that had been stolen by Callis.

Another of Callis' customers was Sir John Wogan of Picton Castle, Haverfordwest, who was an officer in the navy, and a former Sheriff of Pembroke; he was said to sell guns to local pirates.

Eventually, the Cardiff pirates were caught; Callis was probably hanged in Wapping, and two other pirate captains, Robert Hickes and Battes, were also hanged. London was determined to deal with the worst area for piracy in the kingdom. In March 1577, the Vice-President of Wales and the Marches was ordered by Elizabeth I to appoint a commission to look into 'certain disorders committed by pyrates' in Glamorgan and Monmouthshire. On 3 April, two commissioners, Fabian Phillips and Thomas Lewis, the Mayor of Cardiff, reported that they had made inquiries into the activities of up to sixty pirates and those who supported them in Cardiff. They added that they strongly suspected that Sir John Perrot, Elizabeth's brother-in-law, and Nicholas Herbert, the Sheriff of Glamorgan, were heavily implicated in piracy. Herbert was summoned to present himself before the Privy Council but he refused to go, saying that he had to be present at the Easter Assizes. But he was ordered, straight after the Assizes, to travel to London, to answer to the charges made against him. In the same year, Vice-Admiral William Morgan refused to help the commission into piracy in the area.

The supporters of the pirates, under the leadership of Nicholas Herbert, challenged the law by saying that there was no difference between taking goods that had been 'taken at sea and those that had been taken on land', that is, that they had the right to keep them. In June 1577, the Privy Council ordered the Judge of the Admiralty to contact the Attorney-General and the Solicitor-General, to decide on the legal situation, and to form a new act, if one was needed. During the same month, Lord Walsingham wrote to the Attorney-General, asking him to hurry with his answer to the Council on how to deal with those that supported pirates in Cardiff.

Some of the Cardiff pirates' backers in Cardiff were ordered to travel to London, to appear before the Privy Council, and early in 1578, six of the leaders, including the Sheriff of Glamorgan, were fined between £10 and £20 and warned that they would be imprisoned if they persisted in trading and supporting the pirates.

Pembrokeshire

The Privy Council had complained in January 1577 to Sir John Perrot (1527–1592) of Haroldston, Pembroke, Vice-Admiral and Sheriff of Pembroke, Member of Parliament for Pembroke and the mayor of Haverfordwest, of piracy off the Pembrokeshire coast, and, specifically, of giving lodging to John Callis. He was also accused of arresting unimportant pirates but allowing people like Callis to escape.

In 1547, Sir John Perrot was warned by letter that pirates were not only receiving lodging, food and drink from him, but also selling their booty openly on the streets of Cardiff, and, in 1522, the Admiralty insisted that he send to London the pirate Philip ap Rees, who, with a Spaniard called John de Andreaca, had attacked ships in the Bristol Channel. But Perrot did not comply; instead, he arrested William Rogers of Herefordshire and Captain Thomas Harys, who had seized ten Flemish ships and had brought their booty to Pembroke to be sold. In 1554, the Admiralty asked Perrot to capture a pirate called Captain Jones, and, in 1556, he was ordered to go to London to explain why he had not arrested the pirates Peter Heall and Philip ap Rees, who had brought a Breton ship to Tenby, to sell the goods. Sir John Morgan, former Sheriff of Pembroke, did arrest the pirates but he sold the cargo, and shared the proceeds with Perrot.

In 1575, Perrot was made chief commissioner, and instructed to get rid of pirates, and by 1579, he had five ships under his command, trying to stop Spanish ships from landing in Ireland.

Around 1576, the pirate Robert Hickes came to Fishguard, mainly because Perrot's agent, Morgan ap Hywel, was the Mayor of Pembroke. He had seized a ship called the *Jonas* off Land's End; she was on her way from Königsberg to Lisbon with a cargo of wheat, rye, gunpowder and timber. It is said that he was able to unload the ship openly, due to 'Vaughan, the Vice-Admiral'.

Hickes was in Milford Haven for five weeks, selling the goods to customers from every stratum of society, from a priest called Andrew, who bought wheat for the winter, to George Devereaux, the uncle of the Earl of Essex, who bought a hundred casks of rye for export to Spain. Sir John Perrot had sent his men on board the ship, to help with the accounting, and he himself bought wheat, which he sent to Galicia to be sold. When nothing was left of the cargo, Hickes sold the ship to Perrot for £10.

Perrot profited substantially from piracy over the years, and with the money he made, he built a huge mansion at Haroldston, and rebuilt the castles of Laugharne and Carew.

Carew Castle

Laugharne was also a safe port for the area's pirates, as were Haverfordwest, Tenby and Cardigan, with the pirate captains frequently staying with Perrot's agents in these ports.

In 1582, Perrot was in Newfoundland, where he and Henry Oughtres attacked Spanish and Portuguese ships and pillaged their cargoes of fish – the first record of piracy in this part of the world. In 1591, Perrot was accused of treason and sentenced to death. But although it was Elizabeth's intention to pardon him, he died in the Tower of London, aged 65.

Swansea

There is a record of an interesting incident that took place in Swansea in 1581. The *Primrose* of London landed in Mumbles to buy coal from the Neath coalmines, but there were rumours that the captain had been trading with the pirate Haynes. The captain was arrested and an inquiry was held, but it was decided that there was no truth in the rumours. Such was the captain's joy on being released, that he gave presents to the important people of the area. Sir William Herbert received a monkey, Sir Edward Mansell received a monkey and a parrot, and even the government's searchers each received a parrot. It is still not known if the captain had been dealing with pirates.

4. Raiders of the high seas

Why are there so many stories about pirates in the West Indies and the Caribbean? There were two main reasons. The seventeenth and eighteenth centuries were periods of great development in the newly discovered continent of America. Many colonies had been established there, the English mainly in the north, and the Spanish in the south, but it was the Spaniards who had received the best deal because they were in possession of lands full of treasures, the treasures of the native inhabitants as well as gold and silver mines, and these treasures were transported back to Spain. Fish, hides and timber were the main exports from the north.

The situation between Protestant England and Catholic Spain was volatile, and the European quarrel spilt over into the New World. Official or semi-official ventures to the New World were the first British voyages, undertaken with the intention of claiming new lands before the Spanish arrived. And these adventurers missed no opportunities to try to steal the Spanish treasures.

As the colonies developed, trade became more and more important and many a sailor ventured to these faraway lands to make his fortune. The treasure-laden galleons were too much of a temptation for some captains and their crews, and if they had not actually had instructions from London to attack these ships, there was nobody there to stop them.

The Caribbean was ideal for piracy. There were numerous islands and secluded bays there, where they could land, to rest, to get fresh water, to hunt game, and to maintain or careen their ships, and it was very difficult for the authorities to find them in this vast area.

Before then, after the death of Henry VIII, in 1547, pirates had been given a free hand to seize ships around the coasts of Britain. Thomas Seymour, who was not only the brother-in-law of the king's widow, but also the Lord High Admiral, profited enormously from piracy, even seizing the Isles of Scilly, which were used as a base for his activities. It was no surprise, therefore, in this political environment, that few pirates were caught. During the 1550s, 1560s and 1570s, no pirate of importance was caught in the ports of Wales.

Because of the threat from Spain, in the period immediately after the Spanish Armada (1588), England strengthened its navy and, by the 1590s, it was difficult for pirates to operate along their home coasts. Therefore, they had to move further afield to look for ships to plunder. Many went first to the coast of Spain, then, to West Africa, and later, to the West Indies. The ships' captains were mainly the sons of the gentry, looking for adventure and hoping to make their fortunes, to enable them to live in the manner to which they were accustomed. Amongst these pirate captains were many Welshmen:

Morgan Matthew

Matthew came from a prominent family from Rhayader, St Fagan's and Llandaff. In 1548, he was off the Spanish coast with two ships, *Mathewe de Kerdiff* and the *Valentine*, under his command, when he attacked a Breton ship carrying the servants of the Portuguese Ambassador to France, as well as items for the embassy. The pirates looted six tables, and many items of silverware worth about £220. Although the pirates were prosecuted, they were able to keep their booty and were pardoned in 1551.

Tomos Prys (1564?–1634)

Born in Plas Iolyn, Ysbyty Ifan, Denbighshire, around 1564, Tomos Prys was the son of Dr Elis Prys, who had close contacts with the political and ecclesiastical leaders of England. Before going to sea, Tomos Prys had been Sheriff of Denbighshire and had fought in the English army, in the Netherlands, Germany, Spain, Scotland and Ireland. After his father died, in 1596, he returned to Plas Iolyn, but he found it difficult to settle down. In 1588, he was amongst the soldiers at Tilbury, waiting for the Spanish Armada to arrive, when Queen Elizabeth made her famous speech.

Prys bought a ship – possibly after being influenced by Pyrs Gruffydd of Penrhyn, to whom he was related – and went to attack Spanish and Portuguese ships. Whilst at sea, he wrote a number of *cywyddau*, Welsh poetry in strict mètre. One was titled *Cywydd i ddangos yr heldring a fu i wr pan oedd ar y môr* [Cywydd to show the bother that a man had at sea]

> *Dilynais, diwael ennyd,*
> *Y dŵr i Sbaen ar draws byd,*
> *Tybio ond mudo i'r môr*
> *Y trowswn ar bob trysor.*
> *Prynais long, prinheis y wlad*
> *Am arian i'r cymeriad.*

[For a period, I followed the seaways of Spain across the world, believing I only had to go to sea to find treasure. I bought a ship and raided the land for money.]

Prys returned to Plas Iolyn, to rest from his pirate activities – but not for long. He decided to go to Bardsey. Lewis Morris, one of the famed Morris family of Anglesey, says that Prys built a house in the remains of the old monastery there, but it does not seem that he made much money from piracy off the Llŷn coast, for he returned once again to Plas Iolyn and settled down to the life of a gentleman. It is quite possible that Tomos Prys was the last of the gentry to write poetry in Welsh.

He did not spend all his time in Ysbyty Ifan, for a great deal of his time was spent in the taverns and inns of London, and he composed a *cywydd* to his son, warning him about the place, saying that 'London was hell'. In his later years, he spent much of his time with other pirates at Bardsey, or in the taverns of Llanrwst. He died on 22 August 1634 and was buried in the churchyard at Ysbyty Ifan.

Welshmen with Sir Francis Drake

It is said that piracy started in the Caribbean when Sir Francis Drake and his brother, John, attacked Spanish ships in the area, in 1571. Before then, in 1567–8, Drake had been there with his uncle, John Hawkins, and there were at least four Welshmen with them: Miles Phillips, Richard Williams, Humphrey Roberts and Thomas Ellis. There was no war between England and Spain at the time, but there occurred a number of battles between the ships of the two countries. Hawkins and his fleet were on their way home past west Hispaniola and aiming for the Florida Channel, when they were blown by a great storm towards the west coast of Florida. Some of the ships had to seek shelter in the port of San Juan de Ulua, but the Spaniards attacked them. Many of the crew were captured, including the four Welshmen, and taken to Mexico City.

This was the period of the Spanish Inquisition, and the sailors were dragged before the clerics. Some were condemned to death by burning, others were sent to slave on the Spanish ships, being whipped all the way from the town square to the port, and the more fortunate were sent to work in factories and large houses. Richard Williams renounced his Protestant faith and became a Catholic, and because of this, he was only sentenced to three years in the monastery of San Benito. After he was released, he married a rich Spanish widow and they went to live in one of the Spanish colonies in the West Indies.

Roberts, Ellis and twelve others were sent to the ships, and there they died. Phillips was more fortunate; he had been sent to work in a silk factory, but he escaped and made his way back to England, reaching Poole, Dorset, in 1582 – one of only two out of the two hundred who came home safely.

There were also Welshmen on Drake's voyage of 1585: the captains Mathew Morgan and Robert Pugh, as well as Anthony Powell, were with the fleet when they attacked Santiago, San Domingo, Cartagena and St Augustine. Powell died some time later, whilst pursuing Spaniards, after he had led the attack on St John's Fort, Florida.

Drake returned on the *Pelican*, in 1595, to the Caribbean, and there were once again a number of Welshmen with him. This is recorded in a Welsh poem written by Lieutenant William Peilyn in '*Bagad o Gymru a aethant yn Amser y Frenhines Elsbeth drwy eu Gorchymyn hi i'r Gorllewyn India i ddial ar, ag i anrheithio'r Hispaenwyr*' [A Crew of Welshmen who went in Queen Elizabeth's Time under her Orders to the West Indies and attacked the Spaniards]. Here is a part of that poem, listing the Welshmen present:

> **Capten Roberts** *yw 'r ail Gwr*
> *A fentria'n siwr fal Saison*
> *Neu fal Theseus gnwppa mawr*
> *Fe gur i lae ei 'lynion*

Huw Miltwn *ymhôb mann*
A wneiff ei rann, ar eitha igŷd
Ar ddai Lifftenant ymhôb trîn
Salbri *a* ***Pheilŷn*** *hefŷd*

Robert Billings, Sersiant Huws
Ni wnant druws ar gelyn du
Wil Tomas *a* ***Wil Jones*** *a* ***Hugh***
Wel dyna'r Criw o Gymru.

Pyrs Gruffydd (?–1628)

Another Welshman, who sailed with Drake, as well as with Raleigh, was the son of the Penrhyn estate near Bangor, and the last of the family, probably, to speak Welsh. It is said that he was with Drake in the Magellan Straits in 1577, but he was certainly with captains Koet and Tomos Prys when they attacked a ship off the coast of Africa.

On 20 April 1588, he sailed from Beaumaris on *The Grace*, reaching Plymouth on 4 May, where he joined Drake and Raleigh's fleet on a voyage to attack the Spaniards in the West Indies. In 1600, Gruffydd seized a Spanish ship, the *Sperenza*, and brought her and her cargo of oil, olives and silk to Aber Cegin (near the present day Porth Penrhyn near Bangor). It is said that he had built a tunnel from Penrhyn to Aber Cegin so that he could bring the goods from his ship to his home. He continued attacking Spanish ships, although England was at peace with Spain, and Spain complained to the English crown. He therefore had to flee and, in 1603, he was arrested for piracy in Cork, Ireland. He had to raise a mortgage on his properties to pay the fine imposed on him. But he once again joined up with Tomos Prys to attack Spanish ships, and he was caught in 1616. He lost all his estates this time, in paying the fine. By 1616, he was in prison in London. He died in 1628, and some say that he was buried in Westminster Abbey, but there is no record of this.

This is a ditty sung in Bangor in days gone by:

> *Llwm ac oer y gwela i'r Penrhyn,*
> *Glan y Môr ac Aber Cegin,*
> *Er pan aeth y Capten Gruffydd,*
> *Dros y môr i sbeilio gwledydd.*

[Penrhyn, Glan y Môr and Abercegin is bare and cold,
Since Captain Gruffydd went overseas to plunder countries.]

It is said that, at one time, Pyrs Gruffydd's drinking horn was kept at Penrhyn Castle – an ox's horn with a silver chain and the letters P G on it, but according to the National Trust, who now own the castle, there is no record of the horn. A house which he had built in Aber Cegin still has the letters P G and the date 1598 on it.

Aber Cegin, where Pyrs Gruffydd landed with the Sperenza

Henry Roberts

In 1575, Captain Roberts sailed for Honduras, but, on his way there, he was caught by the Spaniards and dragged before a court of the Spanish Inquisition in Tenerife. He succeeded in bribing a monk, and he escaped to continue his voyage.

In 1581, he seized two Portuguese ships returning from Brazil, and by 1592, he was back in the Caribbean, attacking Spanish ships. In 1595, Roberts, along with a number of other Welshmen, including Captain John Myddleton, were in the West Indies when two Spanish towns, Porto Santo and Santiago de Leon, were captured.

Huw Gruffudd (?–1602)

He was one of three sons of Cefnamwlch, Llŷn; his father, Gruffudd ap John, was a relative and friend of Sir Richard Bulkeley of Beaumaris. Sometime in 1597, a merchant from London asked Huw Gruffudd to be the captain of his ship, the *Pendragon*, which was to carry illegal arms from Plymouth to French and Italian ports in the Mediterranean. He sold the arms in Toulon and Leghorn (Livorno, to give it its proper Italian name) and, sometime later, the *Pendragon* was sold to a merchant from Toulon. Gruffudd returned to England and, in about 1599, he became captain of the *Phoenix*, which went to attack ships along the coast between Brittany and Gibraltar. With the *Phoenix* full of booty, he returned to Wales, arriving at the Tudwal Islands, which were not very far from his father's home. It is said that one of the chests from the ship was so heavy that they had to have two strong horses to drag it on a sledge to his brother John's house.

Gruffudd borrowed a horse and went to Beaumaris, to see his

father's friend, Sir Richard Bulkeley, and, some days later, one of Sir Richard's men appeared on one of the Tudwal islands and sailed the *Phoenix* to Beaumaris. It was just in time, because Captain Morgan of the English Navy arrived soon afterwards and tried to get the inhabitants to say where Gruffudd and his ship had gone. John Gruffudd hurried to Beaumaris, to warn his brother, and the booty was sold before Captain Morgan arrived there. The government issued a warrant for Huw Gruffudd's arrest, but, by then, the pirate was back on the high seas.

He returned to sea with a crew of forty-five, his master and his lieutenant being Welshmen from Swansea. He had christened his new ship *Pendragon*, in memory of his first ship as a pirate. One of the ships he seized with his new ship was the Breton ship *Peteryn*. Whilst searching the ship, he found some French and Spanish money, which had been hidden, and he was sure that there was more money hidden somewhere. As the captain refused to tell him where, a rope was put around his neck and he was raised a number of times from the deck, but he would not tell them anything and no more money was found. Gruffudd and his crew attacked ships along the coasts of Western Europe for two years, and then moved to North Africa.

He became friendly with the inhabitants there and he even had a house in Tunis. In 1602, he fell ill, and an old friend of his, Richard Lamb, moved him to Algiers, to get better medical attention, but he died there. His crew, who were staying in his house in Tunis, were accused of stealing his money and were thrown into prison, but it was Lamb who had taken the money to keep it safe, and he had to use it to pay for the crew to be released.

Gregory Jones

He was the son of another prominent Llŷn family; his father, Sir William Jones, was owner of Castellmarch near Abersoch. In a diary dated 21 February 1645, there is an entry that says that Gregory Jones went to sea as a privateer after the English government had declared war with Spain, and that he paid for equipping his ship himself. When he returned to Llŷn, he was caught in his bed in Castellmarch by officers from a warship and sent, possibly, to Ireland – England and Spain had by then become allies.

Sir Robert Mansell (1573–1653)

He was born in Margam, Glamorganshire, and went to sea when he was quite young. He served under Sir Walter Raleigh, when Cadiz was sacked in 1596, and was subsequently knighted. He was given two ships, the *Hope* and the *Advantage*, and given orders to guard ships sailing from the west towards Dunkirk. In 1602, he attacked six Spanish ships, capturing two, sinking two and damaging the other two.

In 1620, Turkish pirates were kidnapping people from the British Isles for the white slave market, and it was decided in London that this had to stop. A fleet of six of the king's ships and thirteen privateers, under Mansell's command, were sent to attack the Turks. They had little luck in attacking the Turkish ports, but they did succeed in releasing some prisoners, having gained access to the dungeons by dressing up as Turks.

They then successfully attacked Algiers, when explosives were put on the Turkish ships in the harbour, in the dead of night, and then set on fire.

Mansell returned home on 3 August 1621. Later, he became Member of Parliament for Carmarthenshire, Glamorganshire and two seats in England.

The Myddletons

Many members of this Denbighshire family were prominent late 16th century pirates. The first was **Captain William Myddleton** (c1550–c1600), or Gwilym Canoldref, as he sometimes styled himself, of Archwedlog, near Llansannan. He was a poet, soldier, sailor and privateer, and had received his education at Oxford. He also received some of his education from William Salesbury, the translator of the New Testament into Welsh. He fought in the English army in the Netherlands and Portugal, and he is described in 1590 as a privateer, returning with a cargo of pepper from Portugal. In October 1589, he seized a ship from Brazil, which was carrying £2,700 worth of sugar, cotton wool and timber. In 1590, he seized two Portuguese ships carrying herbs and gems from the Far East – a cargo which was worth £25,000.

In 1591, it is said that he 'saved the English fleet which was sent to the Azores to intercept the Spanish galleons'. There is a record also that he was a privateer off the North African coast. In 1595, along with Drake and Hawkins, he went to the West Indies, where they attacked San Juan in Puerto Rico and tried to seize Panama. But the Spaniards were after them. Drake and Hawkins died after catching some disease, and Myddleton was nearly caught off Cuba by three Spanish galleons.

It is believed that Myddleton translated the Psalms into Welsh in 1596, when he was a privateer in the West Indies, and they were published posthumously in 1603. It is said that Myddleton, Tomos Prys and a Captain Koet were the first to smoke tobacco in

William Myddleton

London; tobacco which they had seized from a ship between the Canary Islands and Africa.

John Myddleton (1563–1595?) was captain of the *Moonshine*, and he led raids on European ships in 1586, 1590 and 1591. He also took part in a raid on the Azores in 1586. In 1592, whilst on his way to the West Indies, he attacked a ship off the Spanish coast. Near Cartagena, he attacked a Spanish ship that had run aground, but Myddleton and twelve other privateers were captured. They were later released, probably after paying a ransom, and by 1594, he was attacking ships in the Caribbean. Later that year, he was amongst a band of privateers who captured Puerto Caballos, in Honduras. Later, off Havana, Cuba, he captured a Spanish caravel, but the local Spanish governor went after the privateers and they were captured. They were transported to Spain and never heard of again.

Another member of the family was **David Myddleton** (?–1616), He first sailed to the Caribbean with Sir Michael Geare, who had been a privateer since 1588. By 1596, Myddleton was captain of the *James*. In May 1601, Myddleton again set sail for the Caribbean and, later that year, attacked three Spanish ships off Cuba, bringing two of them back to England. He returned to the Caribbean in 1604–6, 1607–8 and 1609–11. He was drowned off the Madagascar coast in April 1616.

Edward Bulkeley

He was the brother of Sir Richard Bulkeley, and it is possible that he went to sea after hearing about the exploits of Huw Gruffudd. He left England on a ship called the *Bravado*, and sailed for the Bay of Biscay, where he attacked Spanish ships, and ships of other countries, selling their cargoes in Turkish ports along the Mediterranean coast. It is said that he seized cargoes worth over £10,000 from Spanish galleons returning from the New World.

But he reached the Turkish port of Bey at an unfortunate time. Some English prisoners had just escaped in a boat, and the authorities were determined to catch someone else in their place, no matter whom. When Bulkeley and his crew arrived at the port, they were immediately thrown into the dungeons, and the *Bravado* was taken from him. It is believed that Edward Bulkeley died in captivity, because nothing more was heard of him.

Captain John James

He is described as a Welshman, although it is not recorded from where in Wales he originated. He raided ships along the Madagascar coast and, later, off the eastern coast of America. He seized a ship in the Persian Gulf, and in their hurry to find gold, the crew threw bales of straw overboard, without knowing that a great quantity of iron had been hidden inside them. He later sailed for Mayotte, near Mozambique, staying there for six months, before leaving for Madagascar in around 1699. Whilst there, he tried to seize a French ship, but as he got nearer, he realised it was another pirate ship, under the command of a pirate called George Booth. James sailed with Booth for some time, but it is not known what eventually happened to him.

Captain John Bowen (?–1705)

Some say that Bowen was born on Rhode Island, in North America, to a Welsh family. Others say that he was born in Bermuda, his father having been transported to the West Indies after fighting on the Royalist side in the Battle of Saint Fagan's, during the English Civil War.

John Bowen started his career at sea on a merchant ship in America, and after a number of years, he became a captain. But he was caught by French pirates, and they took him with them as they attacked ships along the West African coast. They then went around Cape Horn to Madagascar, where they were shipwrecked and captured. Eighteen months later, the pirates, including Captain Bowen, were rescued by the pirate John Read of Bristol.

Since Bowen believed that he would never see America again, he decided to join Read. Another pirate, the above mentioned

*A cemetery on Reunion, where many pirates are believed to be buried –
including, possibly, John Bowen (Photo: Cynan Jones)*

George Booth, joined them, and within a short period of time, they
had three ships and over two hundred men under their command.
Towards the end of 1700, Booth and twenty pirates were killed in
a battle with Arab soldiers, and John Bowen became captain of one
of the ships, the *Speaker*, which he used to attack numerous ships
off the coast of Malabar.

In 1701, near the entrance to the Red Sea, Bowen seized an
Indian ship with over £100,000 worth (about £90 million in today's
money) of goods on board. But on 7 January 1702, after having
seized several other ships, the *Speaker* went aground on the coast
of Mauritius. The cargo was saved, and Bowen bought a new ship
and left the island in March.

By April 1702, he had returned to Madagascar, building a fort
at St Mary. One night, two slave ships anchored nearby and Bowen

and his men attacked them, whilst the crews were sleeping. After the ships were captured, most of the crew of fifty joined the pirates. Through the rest of 1702, Bowen and his men attacked all manner of ships – from Europe and India – off the coast of Madagascar.

Then, he left New Methelage for Joanna, and reached Mayotte towards the end of 1702, where he joined up with other pirates, including Thomas Howard, who is said to have been a Welshman who had escaped to Jamaica from his creditors. They attacked a number of ships throughout 1703, and, by October 1703, they had 164 pirates with 56 guns under their command. It is estimated that Bowen seized goods worth £180 million in today's money, over a period of two years.

In 1704, Bowen sailed for Reunion, and settled down there, but in 1705, after suffering a stomach complaint, he died in March. It is believed that the stomach complaint was caused by drinking rum from lead containers. It is said that, when he died, he had a million dollar's worth of money on him, but all this was seized by the church – which refused to give him a Christian burial – and the East India Company from which he had stolen so much over the years.

David Williams (?–1709)

Williams was the son of a farmer from north Wales, and whilst an ordinary seaman en route to India, he was inadvertently left in Madagascar. He took part in battles between the island's various tribes and he became friendly with one of the chiefs and was made commander-in-chief of his army of 6,000 men. But he escaped from the island, on the privateer *Pelican*, at the beginning of 1698, and later, in May of that year, he joined the *Mocha*. The *Mocha* attacked a French ship and stole £2,000 in cash from her, and later, in September 1698, they attacked the *Great Mohamed* in the Red

Sea. She was carrying £130,000 in cash, and each crew member received £700.

In September 1699, the crew dispersed in Madagascar, after an English warship arrived there. The pirates were offered a pardon, but each one – including Williams – refused it, and they joined pirate captain George Booth on the *Dolphin*, later capturing a French ship. Towards the end of 1699, the *Dolphin* was caught by a British warship near St Mary's Island, but the crew set her on fire and escaped to Madagascar. There, they joined John Bowen (see above) and Williams sailed with him, on the *Speaker*, until she was shipwrecked in 1701. They returned to Madagascar, where they were caught by the pirate Van Tyle, who was raiding along the coast of east Africa and the Indian Ocean, with a Welsh pirate called Captain James. Some of the crew – including Williams – were forced to work as slaves on a plantation on Madagascar. David Williams was there for six months, before he managed to escape and join a tribe of friendly natives; he stayed with them for a number of months, living in a small settlement, which was under the command of a Dutchman called Pro. In November 1603, Williams and Pro were captured by HMS *Severn*, but they managed to escape off the Comoro Islands, in February 1704.

Williams later joined the pirate Thomas White, becoming his quartermaster in 1707. They attacked two ships in February 1707, near the Nicobar Islands, and then, in August 1707, they attacked five English ships in the Red Sea, seizing £50,000 worth of cash and goods. Williams was by now a very wealthy man, but in January 1708, he was shipwrecked in a storm. The pirates then attacked two pirate ships, the *Greyhound* and the *Neptune*, and stole not only the ships but also their cargoes of alcoholic drinks. Williams was later made captain of the *Neptune*, but he was again shipwrecked, in a hurricane, after he had left Madagascar.

Then, Williams and ten other pirates seized a small ship and sailed to the Mascarene Island, but failed to land there and eventually landed in Mathelage (Majunga today), Madagascar, where he settled, dealing in slaves. But the pirates were later forced to flee, after they offended the local chief. A storm blew their ship to the port of Boyne, which was just a few miles from Mathelage and still part of the kingdom of the chief from whom they had just escaped. Williams and some of the crew left the ship and paddled ashore in a canoe, but the natives were waiting for them and they were caught. They were tortured for a whole day, by having hot ash thrown into their faces and young boys hitting them with sticks. Williams offered $2,000 to the chief for his life, but the chief took the money and refused to release him. Williams was eventually killed with spears, sometime in 1709, bringing thirteen years of piracy to and end. It is said that Williams was a very cruel man and few mourned for him.

Samuel Hopkins (?–1709)

Hopkins was no ordinary seaman, or pirate captain; he was an apothecary. He sailed for the South Seas in August 1798, as an assistant to Dr Thomas Dover. After rounding the Horn, their ship anchored, on 1 February 1709, off the island of Juan Fernandez, and whilst there, he saw a small island nearby. On the island was Alexander Selkirk, whose adventures became the basis for Daniel Defoe's novel, *Robinson Crusoe*. The ship then sailed north, seizing a Spanish ship, and then, in April 1709, they attacked Guayaquil, in Ecuador. Whilst there, the crew caught the plague, after they had slept in a church where the Spanish had buried under the floor those that had died of the disease. Dr Dover and Hopkins worked hard, treating the 180 members of the crew by bleeding them, but although Dr Dover succeeded in saving 169, Hopkins was not amongst them – he was the first to die. But he was not the only Welshman to die there. Dover records that 'Thomas Morgan a Welsh-man, died the 31st of May'.

Tom Collins

Collins was born in Pembrokeshire, and he became a member of pirate Long John Avery's crew, arriving in Madagascar in 1695, on the *Charming Mary*. He then joined the ships of captains Thomas White and Booth, and whilst in Madagascar, it is recorded that he met the Welsh pirate captains John Bowen and David Williams. Whilst with Williams, they were both caught by the Dutch pirate Ort van Tyle, and were kept as slaves, until Collins broke his arm. Later, around 1715, Collins was released and he became a slave merchant, controlling the slave trade in Madagascar for a number of years.

Paulsgrave or Palgrave Williams

Williams was born on Rhode Island, North America; his father was Welsh and the Attorney General of the state. The son was a goldsmith by trade, and that is possibly how he heard about Spanish galleons, full of treasure, which had sunk after leaving Panama. Williams bought a ship and employed pirate Black Sam Bellamy to go to look for the sunken galleons. With them were two men of Welsh descent, the captains Evan James and Henry Jennings. But the Spaniards had been there before them, and they later learnt that the cargoes were being kept at Barra de Ays, on the Florida coast. Jennings and three hundred men – but without Williams – set out for the town and seized 60,000 pieces of eight – 250,000, some say.

Williams had spent a considerable amount of money trying to

get the treasure, and, therefore, he turned pirate to try to recoup his outlay. Over the next fifteen months, Williams and Bellamy seized over fifty ships. One of these was the French ship *St Marie*, which was at anchor off the Cuban coast. Four ships under the command of Williams, Jennings and Bellamy sailed into the bay, with the pirates stripped naked – 'all in their skins or buff with naught on but their cartridge boxes and naked cutlasses and pistols'. The ship was captured but there was nothing of value on her, except some French linen, but the captain was tortured and he eventually told them where 30,000 pieces of eight were hidden. Jennings left to find a friend of his, Captain Benjamin Hornigold, but when he returned, Williams and Bellamy had left with all the money.

In the spring of 1717, Williams and Bellamy decided to return home to North America, attacking a number of ships on the way. After they reached New England, Williams visited his mother and sister. He then sailed further north, meeting Bellamy once again, off the coast of Maine, where they attacked a number of ships, including one carrying a cargo of 70,000 bottles of Madeira wine. They had, on average, attacked a ship every fortnight.

As he was now a very rich man, Williams decided to return to his wife and children in Newport, Rhode Island, whilst Bellamy went to Cape Cod, where he was caught in a great storm on 26 April 1717, and his ships, the *Fisher* and the *Whydah*, sank, drowning Bellamy and his crew of 144. Williams heard about the sinking, and he sailed to the area, two days later, to try to save some of the booty, but to no avail.

Later, Williams attacked two ships and then sailed for Cape Cod, where, on 6 July 1717, he arrived to sell his cargo – and that was the last anyone heard of him.

Thomas Davis (1695–1717)

Davis – a Welshman, according to contemporary records (it is believed that he was born in Carmarthenshire) – was a carpenter on the *St Michael*, and when Black Sam Bellamy seized the ship, he insisted that Davis became a carpenter on the *Whydah*. It is said that Davis was none too happy to join the pirates, but after Bellamy promised to release him as soon as he found another carpenter, he agreed. But Bellamy did not find one, and Davis was on the *Whydah* when it sank off Cape Cod. Davis, along with a half-Indian called John Julian, were the only two from a crew of 146 to survive, but he was captured and dragged before a court in Boston, where he was accused of piracy.

In court, there were several who gave him glowing testimonies, one from an ex-employer, who said that he had 'a good education in a religious and orderly family, and that his conversation, carriage and behaviour all that while was very decent and becoming". Davis was subsequently found not guilty of piracy.

Robert Beaver (1748–1852?)

Beaver was born in Aberffraw, Anglesey, in 1748. He went to sea as a young boy and, within a few years, he was made captain of his own ship, trading in linen, wool and cotton, as well as sugar and slaves. In 1778, when he 30 years old, he received a letter of marque from the English government to attack French and American ships. He was now captain of the *Juno*, a ship with 24 guns, and later became captain of the *Hero*, which had 28 guns. In October 1782, after seizing over fifty ships and becoming a very rich man, he retired from the sea. He settled in Amlwch, on Anglesey, got married and had eleven children (some say twenty-three), and he

Captain Henry Morgan c. 1670

became the lighthouse keeper on Point Lynas. It is said that he was 114 when he died.

Captain Morgan, later Sir Henry Morgan (1635?–1688)

It is said that Henry, or Harry, Morgan from Monmouthshire was the most successful of the eighteenth century pirates. He reached Jamaica in 1655, with Cromwell's army, and stayed there, leading raids against Spanish ports in Cuba, Panama and Venezuela. He had up to a thousand men under his command, and it is said that he stole a million pieces of eight.

But he was not the first of the Morgan family to become a pirate. **Colonel Bledri Morgan** was one of Jamaica's leading pirates between 1660 and 1670, and, in 1661, he had 300 men under his command, when he attacked Panama. In May 1671, he was made Deputy Governor of Providence Island.

Henry Morgan's uncle, **Lieutenant-Colonel Edward Morgan** (?–1665), was also a Caribbean pirate. He had served as a mercenary in Germany, and he was a colonel with the Royalists during the English Civil War. When Charles I lost his throne, Morgan escaped to Germany, returning when Charles II was proclaimed king, and was appointed Lieutenant-Governor of Jamaica, reaching the island in 1664.

In 1665, England and Holland went to war against each other, and Morgan was commissioned to lead a fleet of privateers to attack French ships and islands held by the Dutch. Edward Morgan had ten ships and 600 men – many of them pirates, who had been released from prison, to sail with him. The captain of one of these ships, the *Speaker*, was another Welshman, Morris or Maurice Williams, but, by this time, Morgan was getting on in years and carrying too much weight, and during the attack on St Eustatius in July 1665, he suffered a heart attack and died.

There was also another Morgan involved with this attack, although he was not related to Edward Morgan. **Lieutenant-Colonel Thomas Morgan** ruled St Eustatius after it was seized, and also the nearby island of Saba. In 1686, he went to assist English forces in St Kitts, who were being attacked by the French, and he was shot in both legs.

In a book published in 1725, Henry Morgan was described by a former Dutch sailor of his, called Esquemeling, as a 'murderous brute' and a 'depraved, vicious, treacherous, almost unparalleled human brute ...' and many other similar names. The author most probably wanted to impress the Dutch and Spanish authorities, who were at war with England. In 1684, Henry Morgan took the publishers to court for libel and won his case – the first recorded successful libel case. The publishers included an apology in subsequent editions, adding that Henry Morgan was a 'gentleman's son of good quality'.

Henry was the eldest son of Robert Morgan of Llanrhymney, Monmouthshire, and he called one of his plantations in Jamaica

Sir Henry Morgan

Llanrhymney. It is believed that he went to Jamaica with Cromwell's army, around 1655, when he was twenty years old, but some say that he was kidnapped and taken to the West Indies against his will. This is unlikely, as his uncle Edward was already there. As Morgan was a common name in south Wales, he may have been mistaken for someone else, who was taken against his will.

It is quite possible that Henry Morgan went to the Caribbean with the chief of the English Navy, Vice-Admiral Penn, the father of William Penn, who established Pennsylvania. Jamaica was seized from the Spanish, and Morgan spent his first years in the Caribbean, attacking Spanish ships and ports in the area, and, within a short period of time, he was captain of one of the English ships.

By 1659 he was captain of a captured French ship, which he used to attack Santiago del Hispaniola. His force landed near the town and, after fighting their way through thick forest, they attacked Santiago and looted the town. The governor offered 60,000 pieces of eight to save his life and he was freed.

In 1662, Morgan and his ship took part in the assault on Santiago del Cuba. Once again, they landed nearby, before fighting their way through thick forest and attacking the town and its garrison, and then razing them to the ground.

He took part in the attack on Campeache in 1663, which destroyed fourteen Spanish ships. The victors took 150,000 pieces of eight and destroyed property to the value of 500,000 pieces of eight.

After each campaign, the booty would be shared out – King Charles II would get a fifteenth part, the Duke of York, who was the Lord High Admiral, would get a tenth, and the rest would be shared between the privateers. But in 1665, Morgan suffered unrest amongst his crew, who wanted a higher percentage of the spoils, and they refused to sail until their demands were met.

That same year, Morgan sailed his ship to the Gulf of Mexico, to attack Villa de Mosa. He and his men were assisted by the local Indians – who hated the Spanish – to go through the forests, but when they arrived there, there wasn't much to steal. On their return, they were attacked by an army of 300 Spaniards, but although Morgan had only a hundred men, it was the privateers who were victorious.

Then, Morgan sailed south, attacking several Spanish towns along the coast of South America. When he reached Nicaragua, he decided to attack the city of Granada, and he was assisted again by local Indians, who agreed to guide him and his men through the forests and across lakes. It took him five days to reach the city; Granada was seized, and three thousand of its inhabitants fled into the forests; the rest were imprisoned. The privateers spent a whole day looting the gold and silver from the city – but there was more than they and the Indians could carry.

After returning to Jamaica, and still only thirty years old, Morgan was made Vice-Admiral, and in 1688, he was appointed chief of all the Caribbean privateers, or Admiral of the Brethren, as he was known.

In 1667, England signed a peace treaty with Spain, but the English were afraid that the Spaniards were preparing to attack Jamaica. The English Navy did not have enough ships to spare to defend the island; therefore, Henry Morgan was appointed an Admiral and became chief of all the pirates and privateers in the area. Within a short space of time, he commanded twelve ships and seven hundred men. Amongst these, only about four hundred were English (it is not recorded how many of them were Welsh, and it is difficult to say if they had been included amongst the English or not). A meeting of the Council of the Brotherhood was held on a small island off Cuba. Morgan wanted to attack Cuba, but he lost the argument and the decision was made to attack Puerto Principe. It may be that they came to this decision because there were many rich merchants living in this port. The ships were anchored in a small bay, and Morgan and six hundred of his men marched through the forests and attacked Cuba's then second largest town, which had eight hundred men defending it. After a battle that lasted four hours, the defenders on the wall were defeated, and the town was seized. The inhabitants were imprisoned in two of the town's churches, but the privateers did not get much booty, although they tortured many. A ransom was demanded for the prisoners, but Morgan heard that a Spanish force was on its way to recapture the town. His men took five hundred cattle, slaughtered and salted them, carried them to their ships, and sailed for Hispaniola, before the Spanish soldiers arrived. When Morgan returned to Port Royal, he was warmly welcomed, especially as he had returned with three more ships than he had had when he left.

Over the following years, Morgan attacked Spanish ships off the North American coast. His ships stopped the Spanish forces in Florida from joining those in Texas, and it can be argued that

Morgan's activities enabled the English, rather than the Spanish, to colonise inland parts of the continent.

In 1668, Morgan turned his sights towards Puerto Bello (Portobello), where Spanish galleons full of treasure gathered before sailing to Europe. There were four forts guarding Puerto Bello, and Morgan knew that he could not sail into the port; therefore, he decided to land 120 miles to the west. He had not told his men (or the authorities in Jamaica) what his target was, in case there were spies in their midst, and when he told them where he was going to attack, many refused to join him, and only 250 men followed him. He gave his men a fiery speech, to prepare them for battle, a speech that was turned into song and sung by many generations of sailors.

> If few there be amongst us,
> Our hearts are very great;
> And each will have more plunder,
> And each will have more plate [i.e. booty].

The men were transported along the coast in 23 canoes and landed a few miles from the port. They first attacked the fort of San Jeronimo, and after a bloody battle, 74 of the 120 defenders of the fort were killed. The second and third forts were captured without much fighting, but many of the pirates were killed, whilst attacking the fort of La Gloria.

By now, Morgan's ships had reached the harbour, and over the next fifteen days, Morgan's men plundered the town. It is said that Morgan had locked the women in one of the buildings, to keep them safe from his men. Although Morgan and his men had taken vast quantities of pieces of eight and tons of gold, they insisted that a ransom of 100,000 pieces of eight was paid, before the inhabitants were released. The inhabitants did not have much choice, as Morgan's men had just defeated a force of 3,000 Spaniards, who had been on their way to relieve the town.

Morgan returned to Port Royal with 500,000 pieces of eight, 300 prisoners and a fortune in gold, silver and gems. Morgan received five per cent, his captains 2,000 pieces of eight each, and each of his men 400 pieces of eight.

In 1666, whilst on one of his ships, the *Oxford*, planning to attack Cartagena, gunpowder in the hold was fired accidentally, killing not only French prisoners which were on board, but also some of his captains. Morgan escaped unharmed.

Although he took the Frenchmen's ship to replace the *Oxford*, he decided against attacking Cartagena, and turned his sights towards Maracaibo, on what is today the coast of Venezuela. He sailed up the gulf towards the port and fired at the forts that were guarding Maracaibo; although they had to fire at one fort for a whole day, the other forts yielded without too much trouble. Morgan and his men reached the town, but most of the inhabitants had fled to the forests, such was the reputation of the 'conqueror of Portobello'.

Although they searched the town high and low, they found only a small amount of booty. Therefore, they decided to attack Gibraltar, which was a hundred miles inland from the Venezuelan coast. A slave, who had been released from the Spaniards, told Morgan that there was a galleon full of gold in its harbour, and that he knew which one. Two hundred pirates went up river to attack the galleon, whilst Morgan and another 250 went to capture the governor, who was on an island in the river. But they failed to capture the governor, and the galleon that they had seized had no gold aboard. And, to make matters worse, there was a Spanish fleet at the mouth of the Gulf of Venezuela, to stop Morgan's ships from escaping to the open sea. Morgan tried to bargain with the Spaniards;

he offered to release the prisoners – but not the booty – if he and his ships could leave. The Spaniards refused, but the delay had given Morgan time to plan his escape. He prepared a fire ship and sailed her towards a Spanish warship. He then attacked the other ships; one was captured whilst the other went aground.

But his problems were not yet over; Spanish soldiers had occupied forts along the river and could fire at his ships. Sixty pirates lost their lives trying to capture one of these forts, therefore, Morgan changed his tactics. Throughout the following day, he arranged for canoes to travel from his ships to the shore, giving the impression that his men were going to attack the forts from ashore. The Spanish turned their guns to point inland, and that evening, Morgan and his ships sailed out into the open sea. He landed in Port Royal on 17th May, with booty worth 250,000 pieces of eight, including slaves and prisoners.

Towards the end of 1670, Morgan and a thousand men decided to try to seize Old Providence. But rather than attack the town, he asked the governor to surrender – and that is what he did. Not one gun was fired, and not one of the 190 pirates or the 270 inhabitants was injured. No prisoners were taken, no one was tortured or raped and very little looting took place, and there was talk for years in the Caribbean about Henry Morgan's civilised methods.

One of his greatest exploits was crossing the Isthmus of Panama with over a thousand soldiers and pirates and attacking Panama City, the most important gold trading centre on the Pacific coast. On the way there, Morgan lost many of his men, due to attacks by small bands of Spaniards and Indians. They had not brought provisions with them, hoping to steal some on the way, but the Spaniards had burnt everything of use in the settlements along the route, and Morgan's army became very short of food.

There were 2,400 soldiers waiting for them in Panama City, and the governor had sworn an oath in the cathedral that he would defend the city till death. On the 21st January 1671, Morgan and his forces attacked the city. After fierce fighting, they captured Panama City. Whilst the Spaniards lost 400 men, Morgan only lost five. The Spaniards tried to put the city to flames, but Morgan's men succeeded in containing the fires, enabling them to loot the buildings. But one of the Spanish galleons had succeeded in leaving the harbour, and it is believed that it was full of gold, as the privateers did not get as much booty as they had anticipated.

After returning to Port Royal, the spoils were shared out as follows: King Charles II got ten per cent, the Duke of York a fifteenth, and Henry Morgan one per cent, which was about 7,500 pieces of eight. Many of the men complained that they had only received two hundred pieces of eight, but Morgan's reply was that there were many injuries, and that the 'compensation payments' were substantial.

Unfortunately for Morgan, during the attack on Panama City, England and Spain had come to an arrangement not to attack each other, and Morgan was ordered to return to London, to face a trial. When he arrived, the stories of his exploits in the Caribbean had arrived before him and he was treated as a hero. He was in London between 1672 and 1674, waiting for his trial, and he spent most of his time between the grand houses and the taverns and brothels. In November 1673, he was called before Charles II, to try to justify his actions in the Caribbean. He must have succeeded (had not the king profited greatly from Morgan's efforts?), for, on 24th January 1674, he was knighted and made Deputy Governor of Jamaica. Nearly a year later, on 8th January 1675, he left London for the Caribbean.

But the relationship between Morgan and Governor Lynch and Lord John Vaughan, who was on the council of the island, was not a good one, and, in 1676, Morgan was once more facing a trial, this time on the charge of conspiring with the French, but by 1677, it was decided that there was not enough evidence against him.

He was later made Governor of Port Royal and, in 1680, Governor of Jamaica. Surprisingly, he tried to end piracy in the region, by offering a pardon to pirates. Some accepted, others refused, and those that continued in their old ways, when captured, were executed. Although he had accumulated great sums of money – it is estimated that Morgan had stolen about one million pieces of eight between 1669 and 1671, he was by now in debt, mainly because he had spent so much during his time in London. It is possible that he tried to end piracy in the area, so that he could make some money by trading legitimately.

Henry Morgan was very fond of alcoholic drink, especially rum (and there is a brand of rum named after him; up to the 1980s, it had his coat of arms on the bottle's neck, with the Welsh word 'Undeb' [union] on it). 'His drinking bouts swelled his belly so as not to be contained in his coat,' said one contemporary report, and in 1688, he died of the dropsy, caused by drinking too much alcohol. Such was the respect for Henry Morgan, that all the guns in Port Royal harbour fired a salvo as a tribute to him.

On the 7th June 1692, the area suffered from a great earthquake, and a large wave swept the Port Royal cemetery into the sea and with it went Henry Morgan's body.

This is only a short account of Henry Morgan's exploits. For a more detailed account, there are many books available – see the Bibliography at the back of the book.

Edward Davis

One who was with Henry Morgan in the attack on Panama City was Edward Davis. He later joined Captain James Cook and it is said that he buried substantial treasure on the Cocos Island. After attacking ships in the Caribbean, Cook rounded Cape Horn in a Danish brig, the 36-gun *Bachelor's Delight*, which he had captured. He then attacked a number of ships on the Spanish Main, and when Cook died of fever on the Galapagos Islands in 1684, Davis – who had been his quartermaster until then – became the captain.

Later, he joined captains Charles Swan and John Eaton, leading a band of up to a hundred pirates. They attacked ships and looted towns along the coasts of Chile and Peru, and Davis had the reputation of being merciful with the crews of ships that he captured. In May 1685, they were lucky to escape from a disastrous battle with the Spanish Fleet in the Bay of Panama. It is said that he had stolen about 50,000 pieces of eight and much gold, silver and jewels.

The pirates then retreated to the Cocos Island, dropping anchor in Chatham Bay, one of the two anchorages on the island. Nobody lived on the island at the time, and Chatham Bay and its sandy beach provided an excellent place to careen or maintain the ships. It was also an opportunity to share the booty, and such was the amount of money stolen that it was shared out, not coin by coin, but by the jug, with each pirate getting $20,000.

Later, Davis and the two captains, with two of their most trusted officers, brought a number of chests ashore in a small boat. Above the bay are steep cliffs, about a hundred feet high, with caves in them, and between the cliffs and the sea are jungle and deep ravines. Was treasure hidden in the caves? No one knows, but many have been looking for it, over the centuries.

The pirates then left the island; Davis went around Cape Horn and on to Chesapeake Bay, on America's east coast, where he received the king's pardon – which was available to all pirates at the time, and he bought land in Cape Comfort, Virginia.

But, by 1702, he'd had enough of the quiet life and he bought a ship and sailed away. He is reported to have attacked Tolu and Porto Bello, although he did not get much booty. It is said that Davis was a pirate captain for longer than any one else, apart from fellow Welshman, Black Bart.

Abel Owen (?–1701)

He was a member of Captain Kidd's crew on the ship *Adventure*. There is reference to Abel Owen in the Welsh novel, *Madam Wen*, by W D Owen, although there is no record of Owen raiding the Welsh coasts, as is referred to in the novel. The novel says that he was a Welshman, but no other source mentions this. Owen surrendered in New York, at the same time as Kidd, but they were not pardoned, as they had hoped. The pirates were taken to London and, after being found guilty at the Old Bailey in 1701, they were hanged at Execution Dock, Wapping.

A Jennings

According to the author Philip Gosse, Jennings was a 'Welsh pirate [who] had been a man of good position, education, and property before he took up piracy, which he did for the love of life and not from necessity'. In 1714, a Spanish fleet of ten ships, on the way home full of treasure, went into difficulty in a hurricane, and was blown onto the Florida shore. While the Spaniards were trying to save the cargo, Jennings and his men attacked them and stole the treasure.

He then sailed for Nassau, in New Providence, and established his headquarters there. He was joined there by other pirate captains and, at one time, there were 2,000 pirates and those living off piracy living there. Jennings was later made unofficial mayor of Nassau and, in 1717, he chaired a meeting on the island, to discuss King George's offer of a pardon to pirates. Jennings and about 150 pirates accepted the pardon, although many returned to their old ways, but not Jennings. He lived in considerable luxury in Nassau.

Hywel Davis (?–1719)

He was born in Milford Haven and went to sea as a young boy. He was on the *Cadogan*, sailing from Bristol to Barbados as an ordinary seaman, when the ship was attacked by pirate Edward England, off the coast of Sierra Leone. The captain of the *Cadogan* was killed in the skirmish. Davis was offered the opportunity to join the pirates, but he replied that he would rather be shot. His answer pleased England, and he was offered the captaincy of the *Cadogan* and ordered to take the cargo to Brazil to be sold.

Davis arranged a meeting of his fellow sailors, but they refused England's offer and insisted that Davis sail the *Cadogan* to Barbados. When they arrived, Davis told the authorities his story, but they did not believe him and threw him into prison.

He was released after three months, without being charged, but he could not find work anywhere. He decided to go to Providence, which was well known as a centre for piracy, as he had decided that, if he could not get legitimate work, he might as well become a pirate. But it was not as a pirate that he was employed by Governor Rogers, who had two ships, the *Buck* and the *Mumvil Trader*. He was employed as an ordinary seaman. Many of the crews were former pirates and, when the ships, full of precious cargo, reached

Martinique, Davis and the crew of the *Buck* mutinied and, later, the crew of the other ship joined them. Fifteen of the sailors held a meeting on the deck of the *Buck* 'over a large bowl of punch' and Davis was elected captain. He drew up the Ship's Articles, which were signed by all the men, and he sailed the *Buck* to Coxton's Hole, on the eastern side of Cuba.

He then sailed for Hispaniola, where they attacked and seized a French ship. They then saw another ship sailing in their direction, and they soon realised that it was a 24-gun, French man-of-war. She was too big for the *Buck* to attack her by conventional means; therefore, Davis sailed towards her, with the sailors that he had just captured lining the deck. The captain of the French warship, thinking it was another French ship, let the *Buck* come up close and, by the time the pirates started shooting, it was too late, and they soon surrendered. Davis and his men looted the French ships, before sailing north, where they seized a Spanish sloop.

They then, in early 1719, sailed to St Nicholas; when they arrived, they flew the English flag, making the Portuguese believe that they were English privateers. They received a warm welcome and they spent five weeks there, careening the ship. This was the process of keeping the hull of the ship clean of barnacles and other things that clung to it, to allow the vessel to move swiftly through the water. Pirates would spend a lot of time careening their ships, in isolated bays and creeks, to ensure that they were faster than the merchant ships. In the warm, tropical seas, this task had to be done every three months.

Such was the welcome of the St Nicholas girls, that five of the crew refused to rejoin the ship, when she sailed for Bonavista and, then, for the Isle of May. There, they came across a number of ships and attacked them one by one, not only seizing their cargoes

Hywel Davis

but also many of the sailors, who voluntarily joined the pirates. One of the ships captured was the 26-gun *King James*, and the pirates took her with them to St Jago. But there was no warm welcome there as the governor suspected that they were pirates. They soon left the port, but, later that evening, they returned and attacked the fort. Three of the defenders were killed and the rest fled to the governor's house. A grenade was thrown into the house and, as Captain Johnson said, in his book on pirates, 'which not only ruined all the furniture, but killed several of the men within'.

The rest of the island heard of the pirates' actions and they gathered together to try to stop them capturing the rest of the island. Davis knew that there were not enough of them to fight the islanders; therefore, they retreated to their ship with what they seized, and decided to sail to Gambia Castle on the Guinea coast, where, according to rumours, there were substantial riches.

Before they reached the Castle, Davis ordered most of his crew of thirty to go below deck. Davis dressed himself as a gentleman, to give the impression that he was captain of a merchant ship. With six of his men, he went ashore to meet the governor. He told him that he was a merchant from Liverpool, on his way to Senegal to trade in gum and ivory, but that a French warship had followed them and that they came to Gambia Castle to hide. He also added that he was keen to buy slaves from the governor.

Davis and his crew were invited to return that evening, for dinner with the governor. He accepted the invitation and returned to his ship, but not before he had had a good look around the fort's defences. That evening, before they went to the fort for dinner, each one of them hid a pistol under his shirt, and when they reached the dining hall, they pulled out their weapons and pointed them at the governor's chest. He surrendered immediately. Davis fired a pistol through an open window, as a signal for the rest of his crew to overpower the defenders of the fort. This they did and their flag was raised on one of the towers, as a signal for the men left on the ship to come to the fort, which was captured with no loss of life or injury.

The following day was spent drinking, eating and plundering, but there was not as much money there as they had thought, although there were gold bars there worth £2,000. These, along with everything else of worth – including the fort's guns – were taken.

As they were leaving the harbour, a French pirate, called La Bouse, saw them and, thinking that this was an English merchant ship, he decided to attack it. He fired his guns and raised his black flag; Davis did the same, and the French pirate immediately realised his mistake.

The two pirate captains decided to sail together down the coast. When they reached Sierra Leone, they saw a ship at anchor, and since Davis was the better sailor, it was decided that he would attack her. As he got near, he fired his guns and raised his flag – but it was another pirate; this time an Englishman called Cocklyn.

The three now decided to attack the fort of Sierra Leone. La Bouse's ship went first on the attack, but the defenders were ready for him, and a battle raged for some hours, before the other two ships joined in, forcing the garrison to surrender.

The pirates spent seven weeks sailing down the coast, with Davis by now having been elected the commodore of the three ships, but the friendship was short-lived. One day, whilst the three pirate captains were drinking on Davis' ship, they started quarrelling; the decision was taken to separate, and the three ships sailed away in different directions.

Davis headed for the Apollonia Peninsula, where he attacked two English ships and one Scottish. The next target was a Dutch ship, but it took until nine o'clock the following morning before Davis' crew succeeded in capturing her, losing six of his crew in the action.

Davis took this 32-gun ship, renamed her *Rover*, and took her with the *King James* to Anamboe. There were three ships in the harbour there: the *Hink*, the *Morrice* and the *Princess*, and amongst the sailors on this last ship was one called John Roberts, of whom we shall hear much more, later. Davis attacked the three ships and captured them without much trouble, but some of the crew had escaped to the shore and warned the men of the garrison, who started firing at Davis. Davis sailed immediately from the area, taking the three ships with him, making a total of five ships under his command. He sailed down the coast towards the Portuguese colony of Princes. On his way there, he came across a Dutch ship, which he captured. On board was the Governor of Accra and £15,000 in money and expensive goods.

When he reached Princes, Davis once again gave the impression that he was an English privateer, and he was warmly welcomed and invited to meet the governor, but, suddenly, a French ship appeared in the harbour. Davis persuaded the governor that she had been trading with pirates, and he received permission to board her and seize her cargo.

It was Davis' intention to plunder the island and, in order to do this, he invited the governor to dinner on one of his ships. His plan was to capture him and insist on a ransom of £40,000, but one of the slaves on Davis' ship, who had been captured with the ship in Anamboe, escaped and warned the governor. Therefore, rather than go to Davis, the governor invited him to his residence, and when he arrived, the governor's men were waiting for him. Davis was shot five times, with one shot going into his stomach. He tried to escape, but he was too weak, due to a large wound in his neck. He emptied his pistols towards the governor's soldiers and then fell down dead. Only one of Davis' men managed to flee, and he rowed back to the ships and they fled from the harbour.

*This is only a short account of Hywel Davis' exploits. For a more detailed account, there are many books available – see list at the back of the book.

Black Bart (1682–1722)

John Roberts was born in Little Newcastle, a few miles from Fishguard, Pembrokeshire, in 1682, but around 1720, he changed his name to one that would send shivers down the spine of most sailors: Bartholomew Roberts. It is believed that he left his home when he was ten years old and went to sea. He was a good seaman and, by 1719, he was the third mate on the *Princess*, a ship carrying slaves to the West Indies. During that year, the *Princess* was seized by Hywel Davis, who gave the crew a choice between being marooned ashore and joining him. John Roberts decided to join him and later became one of the world's greatest pirates.

Roberts' talents were soon discovered by his fellow Welshman, and it was not long before he was made first mate, and when Davis was killed in the battle on the West African coast, Roberts was chosen by his fellow pirates to become their captain – only six weeks after he had joined them.

Bartholomew Roberts was a strict disciplinarian, but he was very fair with his crew. Although he dressed as a 'typical pirate', he certainly behaved differently from the other pirate captains. Each member of crew had to swear an oath on a Welsh Bible that they would not quarrel, swear or play cards on board his ship, and lights had to be out on his ship by eight o'clock at night. Roberts was also a religious man, and he would hold services on board. The pirates were forbidden to work on Sundays, neither would he, under any circumstances, attack ships on Sundays. He was a teetotaller, and his preferred drink was tea.

It could also be said that his men respected the church, for when they seized a ship called the *Onslow*, off the African coast, with a chaplain on board and failed to persuade him to join them by offering him a share of the booty, they returned all his possessions to him – apart from three prayer books, which they kept for themselves.

The arrangement was for the booty to be shared fairly between the crew, and each one who had lost an arm or a leg in the fighting would be compensated. Each one could retire when he had saved enough money – which was not the case with every pirate crew. And it is said that Black Bart had a band to play music during battles, to urge the men on. But if anyone broke his rules, they would be punished mercilessly, usually by being hung from the mast and whipped.

Within a few years, Roberts became known as Black Bart, or *Barti Ddu* in Welsh, and he became the scourge of the high seas. But why Black Bart? He is described by Captain Charles Johnson, in his book on pirates, as 'a tall black man, nearly forty years of age'. One can be fairly certain about the facts concerning Roberts' exploits, as they were published in Johnson's book about three years after Roberts' death. No one knows exactly who Captain Johnson was, but many believe he was Daniel Defoe, the author of *Robinson Crusoe*. There are also many documents mentioning Roberts in the National Archive in London.

Black Bart

His first ship was a frigate called the *Royal Revenge*, and he sailed back and forth in her, from the African coast to the Caribbean, attacking most of the ships that he came across. Amongst his greatest exploits was sailing into Bahia harbour, on the coast of Brazil, where 42 Portuguese merchant ships were at anchor. They were waiting for two warships, with 70 guns between them, to escort them to Lisbon. Black Bart sailed into their midst and, when the Portuguese crews saw the pirate, they surrendered immediately. He went to the largest, the *Sagrada Família*, and ransacked her, stealing about £20 million worth of gold and jewellery belonging to the Portuguese king.

Whilst Black Bart was on the island of Dominico, the French

Black Bart's flags

authorities in Martinique heard he was there and prepared two warships to go after him. Black Bart left Dominico and headed for the Granadilloes, and stayed in a lagoon near Corvocco to careen his ships. But the French were after them, and, only a few hours after they had left the lagoon, the French warships arrived. But it was not for fear of the French that the pirates had left; it was the crew's longing for wine and women.

In 1720, he sailed as far north as Newfoundland, and when the sailors there heard that he was coming, such was their fear of him that the crews of 22 ships anchored in Trepassey left their ships and went ashore to hide. Black Bart and his men seized the ships and sank them. He then attacked the buildings on the shore, setting them aflame, and destroyed the plantations and fisheries. The only ship left unharmed was a Bristol galley, which Black Bart took. Fortunately for the pirates, the galley had 16 guns on board, for, when they left the harbour, nine or ten French warships came across them. The pirates sank all the French ships, apart from one with 26 guns, which they took with them; she was renamed the *Fortune*, and the French sailors were left in the Bristol galley.

Over the next few months, Black Bart's crews attacked four English ships: the *Richard*, the *Willing Mind*, the *Expectation* and the *Samuel*. The *Samuel* was a rich prize, with many passengers on board;

they were threatened and, eventually, they gave all their possessions to the pirates. The pirates broke into the holds, and stole sails, guns, gunpowder and £8,000 – £9,000-worth of the most expensive goods. A few days later, Black Bart attacked another English ship, and then an American ship called the *Little York*, and then another two English ships, the *Phoenix* and the *Sadbury*.

They then returned to the Caribbean, but they were less successful here. They decided to go to the town of St Christopher, but there was no welcome for them, and they, therefore, burnt two ships that were in the harbour. They went to St Bartholomew, where they had a better welcome, with the governor selling them provisions and the local girls very glad to see them.

They left there and sailed for the coast of Guinea and, on their way there, they seized a French ship and renamed her *Royal Fortune*, a name Black Bart had used on many of his ships. But they did not reach Guinea, as Black Bart had decided to sail for Surinam, which was over two thousand miles away. They had only one barrel of clean water between 24 sailors, and by the end of the journey, they were only getting a mouthful of water every twenty-four hours, leading some to drink their own urine, or sea water, in desperation, and many of them died. Others died of starvation before the end of the journey.

But they came across three ships, and were given food and drink, and they carried on to Surinam. There, they filled the ship with fresh water and provisions and returned to the Caribbean, heading for Martinique. Black Bart entered the harbour, flying the flag of a merchant ship, and met no opposition. He seized all the ships in the harbour; he put all the passengers in one ship and set the other twenty on fire. It was there that they heard that the French had sent warships after them, a few months earlier.

Black Bart was not happy that the governors of Martinique and Barbados wanted to catch him, and, as well as sinking their ships, he had a special flag made – a black one with a figure on it representing himself standing on two skulls, with the letters A B H and A M H representing the governors of the two islands (A Barbadian Head and A Martiniquan Head). This was the first time that a pirate had used a black flag with skulls on it. Black Bart seized a ship carrying the governor of Martinique in April 1721, and captured and hanged his old enemy.

Then, Black Bart sailed towards Deseada, attacking French and Spanish ships, as well as ships belonging to other nations, and then continued towards the Guinea coast. From there, he crossed the Atlantic towards the African coast, landing in Senegal, which was under the command of the French. Two French warships attacked Black Bart, but they were defeated and the two captured ships were taken by the pirates to Sierra Leone. They then sailed along the coast, attacking numerous ships.

In Calabar, they tried to trade with the natives, but they refused to trade with pirates, even though they were 'without the light of the Gospel, or the advantage of an education ... [but have] ... such a moral innate honesty', as Captain Johnson said in his book. Black Bart sent forty armed men to try to force them to trade, but two thousand native warriors appeared and the pirates had to retreat – but not before putting Old Calabar to the torch.

They then sailed south, seizing a ship called the *King Solomon*, by rowing a small boat towards her, boarding her and seizing her, The next ship to be captured was Dutch, the *Flushing*, and part of the booty on this ship were sausages, which had been made by the captain's wife.

They then sailed to Whydah, where they attacked English,

French and Portuguese ships. One of these was a slaver called the *Porcupine*. Black Bart insisted that the captain pay a ransom before she was released, and he was sent ashore to fetch gold dust, but he did not return, and Black Bart was sure that he was preparing to return with armed men, to seize back his ship. He decided to put the *Porcupine* on fire, but in his hurry to leave, he left most of

Black Bart with the flag

the slaves in chains in the hold, and eighty of them burnt to death. Many others, who had jumped overboard to escape the flames, were eaten by sharks.

Due to his numerous exploits, Bartholomew Roberts became a very rich man. It is said that he had seized over 400 ships in two years, and during his career as a pirate, he had stolen gold, silver and other treasures worth £51 million.

But Black Bart was too successful, and was causing enormous losses to the English merchant fleet. King George offered him a pardon, to try to stop these losses, but Black Bart refused to accept it, and, in February 1722, Captain Challoner Ogle in his warship, HMS *Swallow*, was sent to hunt him down. *Swallow* came across some of Bart's ships in a creek on Cape Lopez, on the Guinea coast. The pirates on the *Royal Fortune* had not noticed that it was an English warship that was approaching, and they decided to attack her, but, this time, the enemy was much stronger than the pirates.

After two hours of fighting, ten of the pirates had been killed and twenty injured, without any losses to the Royal Navy.

The captain of another of Black Bart's ships, the Welshman Skyrme, had already lost a leg in the fighting, and when he saw that the battle was lost, he gathered all his men around the powder magazine. A pirate called John Morris fired his pistol into the powder, causing a huge explosion, but he only succeeded in killing himself and burning many of the other pirates.

HMS *Swallow* then continued up the coast, looking for the *Royal Ranger* with Black Bart on board. When Black Bart first saw the English warship, he thought it was a French ship, and he prepared to attack her rather than defend his ship. HMS *Swallow*, therefore, was allowed to come up close to the pirates and attack them. The English warship fired her guns at close range and, after a fierce battle, Black Bart was shot in his neck, and he died resting on one of the cannons on the deck of his ship. He was buried at sea in his colourful clothes – only two and a half years after he had accepted Hywel Davis' invitation to become a pirate.

★*This is only a short account of Black Bart's exploits. For a more detailed account, there are many books available – see list at the back of the book.*

James Skyrme (1678–1722)

Charles Johnson describes him as 'a Welsh man', although some say he was born in Somerset. In 1729 he was on the sloop *Greyhound* when it was seized by Black Bart. He was given command of the *Ranger* and sailed with Black Bart. He was captured by HMS *Swallow* in 1772. He lost a leg in the fighting and 'fought upon his stump', according to Johnson. He was taken prisoner, with the rest of the crew of the *Ranger*. He was tried at Cape Corso Castle in March 1722, found guilty and hanged.

Peter Scudamore (1686/7–1723)

Born in Wales, he was a surgeon on the galley *Mercy*, which was sailing off Calabar when Black Bart attacked her in February 1722. He joined the pirates, and was caught by HMS *Swallow* at the time when Black Bart was killed. He stood trial at Cape Corso, and part of the testimony against him was that he had stated that he wanted to be the first surgeon to sign pirates' articles voluntarily. He was also accused of trying to seize the *Swallow*, whilst a prisoner on her, when she was sailing to Cape Corso. He had answered an officer on the ship, when asked what he was whispering, "About horse racing." He was found guilty and hanged.

William Davis (1699–1723)

He was an ordinary seaman, born in Wales, who is said to have left his ship in Sierra Leone, after hitting the mate. He went to live amongst the natives, and was given a wife by them, but, one night, he exchanged her for some alcohol. Her relatives were none too happy, and they went looking for him. After he was caught, they discussed cutting off his head, but eventually decided to sell him as a slave. He worked for Seignior Jossee, 'a Christian black and native of that place', for two years. When Black Bart and James Skyrme came to the port in July 1721, he seized his chance and escaped to join them. He was with the pirates when they were caught by Challoner. He was taken to London, where he was found guilty of piracy and hanged.

John Evans (?–1723)

Another pirate who is described in Captain Johnson's book as being a Welshman is John Evans. The book was published a year after

Evans was killed, so we must assume that Johnson is correct. Evans arrived in Jamaica as a mate on a merchant ship. He then became master of a ship that sailed out of the port of Nevis, but this did not last long, as piracy was affecting trade in the area. Soon, Evans was unemployed. The only work available was in the plantations on the island.

Evans and four others decided that this work was too hard, so, in September 1722, they stole a canoe from the harbour at Port Royal and used it to steal from houses along the coast. After a few weeks, they came across a sloop in a place called Dun's Hole. Evans and his companions boarded the sloop, Evans proclaimed himself captain, and then sailed the ship to a small port, where he bought beer for all the crew and everyone that agreed to follow him to attack ships. He spent so much money at the inn that he was invited by the innkeeper to return − this he did. That night, he broke into the inn and stole drink and other goods. He returned to his ship, which he had named the *Scowerer*, and, the following day, sailed out to sea, to seek ships to attack.

The following day, they came across a Spanish ship, which they seized, and such was the booty that each pirate received £150. The ship then sailed for Puerto Rico, where the crew attacked an English ship called the *Dove*. Since the mate of the *Dove* was an excellent seaman, he and three other members of the crew were forced to join the pirates.

On 11 January 1723, the *Lucretia and Catherine* was captured, and then a Dutch sloop, whose booty enabled each pirate to get £150. The *Scowerer* then sailed to Jamaica for careening. When, later, they reached the Grand Caymans, a quarrel started between Evans and his mate. Evans challenged the mate to a duel, but the mate refused. This made Evans angrier, and he started to hit him over the shoulders with a cane, but the mate pulled out his pistol and shot Evans in his head, killing him instantly. The crew members – who had been forced to join the pirates – then attacked the mate, who tried to escape over the side of the ship, and shot him dead.

The crew could not decide who should replace Evans as their captain, so they decided to share the booty of £9,000 between the thirty of them, and they returned the *Scowerer* to Port Royal.

John Phillips (?–1724)

Phillips was a Porthmadog-born ship's carpenter, who was on the *Iven* when she was captured by two of Black Bart's former captains, Thomas Anstis and the Welshman, Thomas Jones. Phillips was forced to join the pirates, who went on to attack ships off Martinique and Montserrat. After seizing a cargo of alcoholic drinks in June 1722, the crew sailed to Mohair Key, to careen the ship and to drink the booty.

Some of the crew wanted to give up piracy, and they wrote a petition to the king, asking for a pardon. Phillips and Thomas Jones took the petition to the governor of one of the islands, and he sent it on to London. They received a pardon but it arrived too late, as the pirates had already decided to continue with their trade. Phillips sailed to London, but when he heard that some pirates had been thrown into Bristol jail, he fled to Newfoundland and found work in the cod industry.

On 29 August 1723, Phillips and other former pirates stole a ship, and the Welshman was elected captain. They attacked a number of fishing vessels, many of whose crews joined the pirates. The ship, which had now been named the *Revenge*, sailed towards Martinique and Tobago, where the pirates again attacked a number of ships. Over nine months in the West Indies, they seized thirty ships – English, French, Portuguese and American.

Sometime in 1724, a member of his crew tried to kill Phillips and persuade the crew to mutiny, but Phillips took out his sword and cut the sailor three times, before he was killed by the other pirates and thrown overboard.

Phillips then sailed back to Newfoundland, to try to persuade those that were working in the fishing industry to join him. Off the coast of Nova Scotia, on 17 April 1724, he seized a ship and captured her captain, Andrew Harradine. Later, Harradine and some of the crew turned against Phillips. In the fighting, Phillips was killed by a blow from Harradine's axe. His head was cut off, pickled and tied to the mast. Some of the pirates who had fought alongside Phillips were thrown overboard, whilst others were jailed in Boston.

The wars between England and Spain, France and Holland came to an end, and their navies started to co-operate against the pirates. The merchants in the various ports were also becoming less keen to trade with the pirates. Already, in 1717, King George had passed the Act of Grace, offering a pardon to pirates, and many accepted it.

Although the pirates, or privateers, had given substantial assistance to the English crown, their usefulness had passed. The colonists in North America complained about paying taxes, especially as the Royal Navy could not protect their ships from pirates, and trade in this part of the world was growing very quickly. Therefore, the English government invested substantial sums in its navy, in order to protect ships sailing between America and the British Isles.

The golden age of piracy was over.

5. Pirate Miscellany

Captain Morgan's Treasure

As Sir Henry Morgan was the best-known of the pirates, many stories about his hidden treasure have cropped up in Wales. Naturally, one story is connected with his birthplace of Llanrhumney. There is a legend that part of his treasure is buried in the town of Rhymney, near Barracks Street. The American author, John Steinbeck, who wrote a book on Morgan, says that he was born in Bryn Oer farm, and, according to local tradition, Morgan's treasure was buried in an old well on the farm, possibly when Morgan went to London to face trial in 1672. Others say his treasure is buried in a place called Rhymney Patch, at the top of Rhymney Valley.

On the Llŷn Peninsula, it is said that he used to call at Abersoch, when he was on his way from the Caribbean to London, staying in a cottage on the outskirts of the village. This cottage is still there, joined to a house called Tŷ Mawr, near a garden centre.

The house by Abersoch 'where Henry Morgan stayed'

According to tradition, the bridge in Abersoch harbour, Pont Morgan, is named after the pirate, but there was another pirate called Morgan in the area: William Morgan, the agent of John Wyn of Bodfel, who was said to live on Bardsey Island, where there is a cave called Ogof Morgan. There is also an Ogof Morgan near Aberdaron, where, some say, again, that Henry Morgan hid his treasure. There is a tradition on the peninsula that the local Morgan tried to hang himself, but failed and that he lost all his hair. Here is a ditty that used to be recited:

> *Morgan a safiwyd a grogwyd 'n o lew,*
> *Yn sgubor Pwll Defaid y collodd o'i flew.*
> [Morgan was saved from hanging
> In Pwll Defaid's barn where he lost his hair.]

Pont Morgan, Abersoch, named, according to local tradition, after Henry Morgan

Rhos Fynach, Rhos-on-sea – a pub since the twelfth century

There was also another Captain Morgan in the area, sailing out of Pwllheli, so it is said. He was a lieutenant to Captain Robert Nutt, until he gave up the life of a pirate in 1637, when Morgan took over and continued to attack ships in the Irish Sea.

On Mynydd Tir Cwmwd, near Abersoch, there is a cave called Ogof Wil Puw. It is said that Wil Puw was a pirate, who hid his booty in the cave.

It is also said that Henry Morgan stayed in Rhos Fynach, in Rhos-on-sea, near Llandudno, which is now an inn and restaurant, but there was also a family called Morgan in Flintshire, the so called Fighting Morgans, and it is said that some of them were pirates. They were related distantly to Henry Morgan's family in Llanrhumney, and it is quite possible that it was one of the Flintshire Morgan's who stayed at Rhos Fynach.

Black Bart's son's Bible

There are no stories of Black Bart's treasure being hidden in Wales, but, according to Roger Talbot of Bridgend, he has a Welsh Bible, which used to be owned by Black Bart's son. In the Bible are the date 1814 and the names of two towns in America – Coalsville and Dunville, in Pennsylvania. This is part of the script at the beginning of the Bible:

'Horace Thomas the son of Horace Thomas went to sea in 1787. William Horace Thomas brother of the above mentioned Cetor [?] Horace Thomas His Book 1819.'

There are also three with the surname Roberts in the Bible: Rees, William S and William T Roberts, all from Pennsylvania.

Black Bart's son's Bible

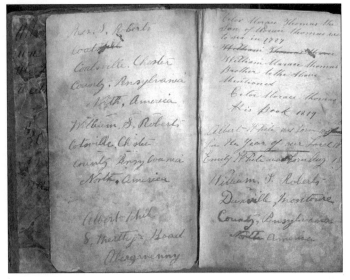

Captain Kidd

As far as we know, Captain William Kidd never visited Wales, but above the door of the Llety Gonest Inn, in Mostyn, Flintshire, is a head of stone. Behind the head is a small goat, or kid, and some say that it is exactly the same as the sign Captain Kidd would put after his name. Before the embankment in front of the inn was built, ships would tie up across the road from the inn. Did the head of stone come from a ship? Did one of Captain Kidd's men come from the area? Captain William Kidd was a Scot, and one of the most prominent pirates of the 17th century. After years as a pirate, he heard that the king was offering a pardon to the pirates, so he sailed to New York and surrendered to the authorities in 1699 – the same year as the inn was built. But there was no pardon for Kidd and his pirates. They were taken to London, found guilty in the Old Bailey in May 1701, and hanged.

Llety Gonest, Mostyn, showing the head above the door

The lady and the pirate

We've already heard of the Bulkeley family of Anglesey as pirates, and of their dealings with pirates, but one of them married a pirate. The pirates were the Bulkeleys of Baron Hill, Beaumaris; it was the daughter of William Bulkeley of Brynddu, near Llanfechell, in the north of the island, who married a pirate.

In March 1735, William Bulkeley and his daughter Mary travelled to Dublin, to see his cousin William Parry. After a few days, William left, leaving Mary with his cousin, and it was then that she met the wine merchant and brewer from Liverpool, Fortunatus Wright. Mary later returned home and, in March 1737, Wright came to Brynddu, to ask for her hand in marriage. William Bulkeley agreed, but he did not have much choice, as Mary was pregnant.

They married on 22nd March, returning to Brynddu on 3rd April, but they didn't stay long in Anglesey, as they went to Liverpool. In the beginning, they would visit Anglesey regularly, but over the years, Wright's visits became less and less frequent – apart from the times he wanted money from his father-in-law. Wright was very cruel with Mary, beating her, say some, but they had six children, although some of them died in their infancy.

Fortunatus Wright was in Italy in June 1742, and there is a record of him taking part in an attack on the town and republic of Lucca, but he was caught and imprisoned for three days. He then moved to Leghorn (now Livorno) in Tuscany.

By 1744, when England was at war with France, he was captain of a privateer called the *Fame*, and by December 1746, it is said that he had captured sixteen French ships, worth a total of £400,000.

One of these ships was carrying the Duke of Campo Florida; Wright seized his property, but had to give it back to him, after pressure from the English government. A few months later, he attacked a French ship carrying goods from Turkey, and once again, he was asked to return the goods, but he had sold them and refused to pay any compensation. He was caught by the authorities in Tuscany, and imprisoned for six months.

During this period, Mary was in Brynddu with her father, and it is very possible that she was much relieved when the war against France ended in 1748. But Wright did not give up seizing ships. He went into partnership with a former privateer called Captain Hutchinson, who had a ship called the *Leostaff*. Hutchinson went to the West Indies and attacked ships there, whilst Wright stayed in Leghorn, to sell the goods seized. As there was no sign that her

A picture of the Fame, *Fortunatus Wright's ship, on the wall in Brynddu*

husband was going to return home, Mary decided to join him, and she reached Leghorn sometime after August 1748, leaving the children in Anglesey with her father. But Wright's fortune did not last long, because there is a record in William Bulkeley's diary that he received a letter from his son-in-law, asking for £300.

By 1756, England was again at war with France, and Wright saw another opportunity to make some money. He got a ship called the *St George*; the government of Tuscany had placed a restriction on her, limiting her to four guns and twenty men, but after she had left the harbour with four merchant ships, Wright took on board another eight guns and fifty five men. And he needed them, for a French privateer was waiting for him, a ship that had sixteen guns and 280 men aboard. Wright engaged the French ship, and, after a battle that lasted an hour, the French surrendered, but Wright failed to seize her, as another two French privateers were sailing towards him.

He returned to Leghorn, and was arrested for deceiving the authorities by adding guns and men to the *St George*, but after pressure from the English government, he was released.

In 1756, William Bulkeley received a letter from his

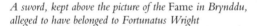

A sword, kept above the picture of the Fame *in Brynddu, alleged to have belonged to Fortunatus Wright*

daughter, saying that a newly-born son had died and that her husband had left her, to attack French ships, and that she was feeling very lonely. About the same time, the King of France and Marseilles merchants had put a price on Wright's head, and he found it difficult to find a port that would allow him to bring his booty ashore. He arrived in Malta with two French ships he had seized, the *Immaculate Conception* and the *Esperance* – worth a total of £15,000, but Malta sided with France and Wright had to flee back towards Leghorn. On the way, he sailed into a storm and Wright's ship sank with all on board.

When Mary received the bad news, she wrote to her father, asking for money, so that she could return home. There is a record in Bulkeley's diary, noting that he sent her two sums of about fifty pounds. But on the way home, the ship carrying her went on the rocks in Cornwall, and her father received a letter saying that she was very ill in Penzance. Once again, her father sent her money. Mary arrived home in Brynddu in October 1759, and there she stayed, being looked after by her father, although her husband, at one time, had been a very rich man.

Hiding and finding pirate treasure

Although John Wyn of Bodfel used to keep his booty on Bardsey, there is a tradition that he kept his money in a pot buried – within sight of seven churches – at y Parciau, Marianglas, on Anglesey. Mrs Griffiths of Hawarden, in a column in the *Daily Post* in 2004, said that her great, great, great ... grandmother had seen a rider on his white horse, galloping along the Marian in Marianglas – John Wyn's ghost, so they say; the rider did not have ordinary feet, but cloven hooves – the sign of the devil. A local midwife had also seen the ghost – which had offered to give her a lift, but she refused.

In 1770, an elderly couple found pieces of gold in cracks in a rock in Bluepool Bay, on the Gower Peninsula. And in 1840, in the same place, two quarrymen came across Portuguese and Spanish moidores and doubloons. As the news spread through the area, many more quarrymen arrived, and they started blasting the rocks, to try to find more coins, but the local landlord, Major Penrice of Kilvrough, near Parkmill, soon came on the scene and stopped them. Was this treasure that had been buried by pirates or did it come from a ship that sank out at sea? It is said that Spanish doubloons were found whilst workmen were excavating the old harbour at Barry, about a hundred years ago, and Spanish gold coins are sometimes washed ashore on Rhosili beach, having come from a ship that sank in the 17th century.

Not every pirate would hold on to his booty. According to tradition, the pirate and smuggler, John Lucas, who lived on the Gower in the 16th century, would share his money with the local people. It is said that his headquarters was an old salt mill in Port Eynon, which had holes in the walls, to enable him and his men to push guns through, to defend the place.

There is a tradition that pirates would stay on Ynys Gron, which is now part of the land reclaimed from the sea by the building of the Porthmadog Cob in 1811. The island was then between the river Glaslyn and the village of Minffordd, and it is said that pirate weapons were found in a cave on the island.

Stealing the pirates' booty

It is said that a pirate ship called the *Deux Amis* was wrecked off Ffynnongroew, in Flintshire. Landlords could claim the cargoes of any ships that were wrecked off their lands, and that is what happened in this instance, but the ship had gone aground on a promontory that separated the lands of two local families: the Talacre Mostyns and the Mostyn Mostyns. They could not agree who could keep the pirates' booty, and after a great deal of quarrelling, they decided to split it between the two families. They also agreed to send armed men to guard the ship and the booty, but they were too late. The locals had been there before them.

Ghosts

It is said that, once every year, a female ghost called Mallt y Nos appears in St Donat's Castle, near Cowbridge, south Wales. It is said that she wears a dark blue gown and has dogs following her. It is said, too, that she is looking for the spirit of pirate Colin Dolphyn, who was burnt to death nearby – or buried up to his neck in the sand, say others, and drowned when the tide came in.

It is said that a pirate stole a silver bell from a hermitage on the side of a cliff in St Govan's, south Pembrokeshire, but as soon as his ship went out to sea, it went on the rocks. The bell was rescued by sea maidens and given back to the hermit. For safekeeping he put it under a rock near a well. It is said that, if the rock is struck, it rings like a bell.

One day, in the spring of 1976, a middle-aged woman took her dog for a walk from the quay at Caernarfon, over Pont Rabar and along Y Foryd, towards Llanfaglan Church. It was a fine morning, with the waters of the Menai Strait gently lapping onto the shore. Suddenly, the woman heard the sound of voices and feet walking towards her. The sound came nearer and nearer and her dog started whimpering. Then, a crowd of colourfully dressed men came towards her; they had silk scarves tied around their heads, wore gold earrings, and each one carried a sack on his back. After they went past her, one by one, they went through the gate to the Llanfaglan churchyard, and she saw each one choosing a grave and jumping into it. She hurried back into town.

Some years later, she told of her experiences to a group of friends, and amongst them was a man in his eighties, who had been born and bred in the town. He referred to the bar across the western end of the Menai Strait, and said that it was very dangerous place, due to the strong current.

"Bodies of those drowned in the Irish Sea are washed ashore near the old church," he said. "Many of them were pirates, and many of the graves have a skull and crossbones on them."

He added that the vicar at the time was too scared not to give permission for pirates to be buried there, in case their friends would attack him. He said that the ghosts of pirates are regularly seen in the area, especially during June.

According to J C Davies, who collected the folklore of Ceredigion in the early 1900s, there was the ghost of a pirate on the bridge that crosses the river Ystwyth, in Llanafan parish. It was the ghost of a pirate who had lived in 'a home for retired pirates' near the bridge, and there was talk also of pirates' treasure being buried near the bridge.

The pirates' bell

Towards the end of the 17th century, Evan Evans established a bell foundry in Chepstow. Most of his bells went to churches and cathedrals, but since it was a very restricted market – they don't often replace their bells, he also started manufacturing bells for ships. Bells were used on board ships in fog, to warn other ships to keep away, and also to warn of a fire on board. A bell is also rung every half hour on board ships, to mark the passage of time.

One of the ships carrying one of Evan Evans' bells was the slave ship *Whydah*. In 1717, the ship was seized by pirate Black Sam Bellamy, and he used her to attack other ships. Bellamy later sailed the *Whydah* to Cape Cod, on the eastern coast of North America, but he was caught in a huge storm, and the ship sank. In 1982, the ship was found at the bottom of the sea – one of the few pirate ships to be found. But although they found plenty of gold in her hold, there was nothing to prove whose ship she was – until, in 1985, they found the ship's bell, engraved with the words: 'The Whydah Galley 1716'.

French privateers drink from St Eilian's Well

During 1702 and 1710, England was at war with France and French privateers sailed along the coast of Wales, attacking ships. In 1707, William Peters, a sailor from Llŷs Dulas, Anglesey, met the boatswain of a French ship in Liverpool. They drank numerous bottles of cider together in the city's taverns, and, at the end of the evening, they decided to meet again, sometime.

At the beginning of January 1708, a French privateer was seen at anchor off Penmon, on the eastern coast of Anglesey. It later sailed up the coast and anchored off Point Lynas, near Amlwch. Some of the privateers went ashore and attacked a tailor's cottage, before stealing a herd of sheep. Others went to St Eilian's Well, to get fresh water, leaving a letter for William Peters under a stone near the well. It is obvious that Peters had told the French boatswain where to get fresh water on the island.

Local people were incensed that a local man had helped the enemy, but William Peters was not a Welshman, he was Dutch and his real name was William Peters Bola.

The capture of Captain Edwards

One who was captured by privateers was Captain Evan Edwards (1747–1829) of Llanfair, near Harlech. In 1780, during the American War of Independence, his ship was seized off Land's End by the privateer *Black Prince*. Captain Edward's brother was also on board; he was put ashore at Looe, Devon, and he travelled to Cork, in Ireland, and then to Fishguard. Captain Edwards was taken to Dunkirk, and a ransom was demanded. The money was paid and he returned home, where, later, he was responsible for building a number of ships on the river Artro, in Pensarn, and at Mochras (also known as Shell Island).

Captain Edwards was not the only one to be seized by American privateers during this time. This is part of a Lloyd's Register report for 1777.

'The following vessels have been taken and ransomed by the Mayflower privateer of Dunkirk … the Nancy … from Jersey to Swansey; the Peggy, Williams, from … Dublin, for 60 guineas each; The Ann, John from Cardigan to Milford, for 50 ditto; the Cardigan, Davids and Plandolen, Evans, from Cardigan to Milford; Briton, Jones, from Dublin to Aberdovey, for 80 each; for 400 the Mary, Griffith, from … to Dublin; … and the Betsey and Valentine, Brigan, from Dublin to Milford, for 130 ditto.'

The raid on Aberdyfi

One afternoon in August 1809 (during the Napoleonic War), a French privateer arrived in Aberdyfi. The inhabitants fled to the hills before the French arrived on the shore, but six of the inhabitants had stayed in the village, and destroyed all the boats on the beach, so that the French could not take them; they also hid every weapon in the village. Four of them left for the hills after the others, but two remained in the village: Gruffudd ab Owen and Rhys. They ran across the beach, towards a promontory that stretched out to sea. It was dark by now, and they could see lights in the distance. They dug two large holes in the sand, and went to hide in them until the French arrived.

Two boats were lowered from the French ship and rowed towards the shore; they were loaded with about a dozen armed men. Before the two boats landed, the French privateer fired towards Aberdyfi. When they landed, the Frenchmen jumped out of the boats and ran towards the houses, leaving two to guard the boats. The French privateers then put the thatched roofs of the cottages on the shore on fire. The two Welsh lads left their holes in the sand, and ran towards the village – each one armed with a gun and a club. When they got near, they crept on their bellies towards the boats on the beach. But when they were about to reach them, one of the guards saw the lads. The Welshmen jumped to their feet and attacked the guards. After fierce fighting, Gruffudd hit one of the guards, who fell unconscious to the ground.

The other Frenchman was getting the better of Rhys, and Gruffudd went to help him just as the Frenchman pulled out a knife. Gruffudd shot him dead. The rest of the privateers heard the shot and hurried back to their boats. Rhys had been injured in the fighting, and Gruffudd placed him in one of the boats, before jumping in after him, but not before grabbing the rope that was tied to the other boat and pulling it with him. He grabbed the oars and started rowing, but two Frenchmen jumped into the water after them. The privateers on the beach started to fire at the two in the boat; one of the bullets hit an oar, and with Gruffudd's weight on it, it broke in two. The two privateers in the water were now near the boat, and Gruffudd hit them with what was left of his oar. One was knocked unconscious, the other returned to the shore. Gruffudd rowed with the remaining oar to a spot about two miles from the village, where he left Rhys with a farmer and went to fetch a band of armed men, to return with him to Aberdyfi.

The privateers were stranded on the beach because Gruffudd had taken their boats, and when the armed men surrounded them, they surrendered. Their ship, out at sea, having seen what had happened on the beach, raised anchor and sailed towards Bardsey.

Gruffudd and Rhys – who soon got over his injuries – were given an award by the government for their bravery in fighting the French privateers.

Celebrating the death of a pirate

Up to the 1850s, on the 3rd of May of each year, the inhabitants of Llantwit Major, near Cowbridge, south Wales, held the Annwyl Festival, to remember the last attack on the town by the Irish pirate O'Neill. He had attacked the town many times before, but on this last occasion, the inhabitants were ready for him. The prettiest girls in the town wore their best dresses, and went to the meadows on Colhugh Point. There, they danced until O'Neill's men were seen approaching. The pirates landed and ran towards the girls, but the men had hidden in gorse bushes on each side of the valley. When the pirates arrived, the men ran down towards them and killed them. O'Neill was captured, tied to a post and set on fire.

What was left of his body was buried on 3rd of May, and this day was celebrated over the years. The inhabitants of Llantwit, Boverton and St Donats would be split up into 'pirates' and 'defenders', with the 'defenders' trying to catch the 'pirates'. Once this had been achieved, they ended the day with running and wrestling competitions, and, then, singing and dancing.

The pirates of Anglesey

It is said that two of the sons of Rhoscryman Bach, near Llanfairynghornwy, in the north of the island, were pirates, who used the nearby Traeth y Fydlyn beach to bring their booty ashore. They were called 'iron fists' and were very unpopular on the island. One had to flee to America, and the other went to work on the ferry that sailed across the Menai Strait. It is said that the one that went to America became a very rich man, and when the news of his death reached Anglesey, a number of people went across the Atlantic, to try to lay claim to his money.

It is also said that Danish or Spanish pirates once landed near Trwyn yr Eryr, not far from Rhoscryman Bach, and that a fierce battle took place there. It is said that many were killed in the battle, and had been buried there.

The *Alabama*

The CSS *Alabama* was an American raider or privateer. She had been commissioned secretly by the Confederate Government during the American Civil War, and had been built in one of the Laird shipyards in Birkenhead. She went for sea trials along the north Wales coast, but a Confederacy crew was waiting for her in Red Wharf Bay, Anglesey, and when the ship was within reach, they rowed out and seized her. They had been staying in John Roberts' cottage on the shore, but they were not going to leave him behind, to tell the authorities what had happened, and so he was taken with them.

Another Welshman who joined the *Alabama* was Samuel Roberts of Caernarfon, who later became known in the area as Sam Alabama. In 1862, he was sailing from Australia to Boston, USA, when the *Alabama* attacked his ship and forced 48 of the passengers, including Roberts, to serve on her. There were five Welshmen on board the *Alabama*: Samuel Roberts; John Roberts, who had been seized from Red Wharf Bay; Thomas Williams and Lieutenant Morris from Caernarfon; and a Hughes from Holyhead. After thirteen months, the *Alabama* went to Cape Town, South Africa, where Sam Roberts managed to escape and return to Caernarfon.

The *Alabama* was sunk off Cherbourg, France, in 1864, after she was attacked by the USS *Kearsarge,* but not before she had sunk over $4 million worth of goods destined for the Union Government. John Roberts of Red Wharf Bay was killed during the fighting, but there is no record of the other three amongst the names of those who were killed or drowned when the *Alabama* went down. Had they managed to escape, like Sam Roberts? There are two other Welsh sounding names on the list: a William Jones, 'born in England', and a David Herbert Llewelyn, an assistant surgeon 'from Wiltshire'; both of whom died during the fighting off Cherbourg.

According to Samuel Roberts, if he had received his due share of the goods seized by the *Alabama*, as was the tradition of pirates, he would have received £2,000 to £3,000, and would have been a very rich man.

Pirates and the Welsh of Patagonia

According to Welsh-Patagonian, Rene Griffith, a singer who sings in both Welsh and Spanish and who now splits his time between Wales and Argentina, his mother was related to pirates. Sometime during the latter half of the nineteenth century, pirates landed in the Welsh colony in Dyffryn Camwy. It is said that they had come from North America, were possibly of Austrian stock, and had deliberately sunk their ship in the area because they knew it was inhabited. It is said that they had plenty of money, and that they built themselves some grand houses. But they were largely shunned by the Welsh as being 'bad people'. Nevertheless, they did marry some of the Welsh women, and one of them – a man called Mariani – was Rene Griffith's maternal great grandfather. It is said that part of the pirates' ship is to be found holding up the roof of a house in Dolavon.

6. Pirates today

Piracy is still a problem in some parts of the world today, not in the Caribbean, but in the Far East – off the coasts of Indonesia and Bangladesh, also off Nigeria and especially along the coast of Somalia where a cruise ship was attacked by pirates in October 2005. But although there was a small drop in the figures for the first half of 2004, there was an increase in the number killed, a total of 30, which is twice the number for the same period in 2003.

One whose ship was attacked by pirates was Michael Hughes of Porthmadog. It was in 1975, and Mr Hughes was on watch at night, on the Blue Funnel ship *Emphasis*, off Bangkok, when he heard a noise. He went to investigate. Ten pirates – some of them armed – came on board, after throwing grappling hooks over the side of the ship. They caught Mr Hughes and tied him up. The second mate came to look for him and he was also tied up. The pirates carried the goods from the ships to their fast launches and disappeared. Mr Hughes eventually managed to untie himself, and freed the mate. They called the captain and first officer, but it was too late to catch the pirates. They were asked to go the local police station, to take part in an identity parade. But the advice he was given was not to identify any of them – although he did recognise three of them as the men who had attacked his ship – in case they retaliated.

Arthur Hughes, originally from Abersoch but now from Rhos-on-sea, was also on board a ship that was attacked by pirates. He was a purser on the *Fort Colonte*, which had anchored off Singapore in 1981, when pirates boarded the ship and tied the captain up before forcing open the safe. There was £50,000 in cash on the ship, ready to pay off the crew, but the money was in a safe in Arthur

Hughes' cabin. One of the ship's cadets came across the pirates, and they fled down the rope ladders that they had placed along the hull of the ship in order to climb on board. Once down the ropes, they jumped into a large canoe with an outboard motor, and disappeared up the coast. After this incident, members of the SAS would regularly sail on board British ships, to stop any attacks, and, according to Mr Hughes, a few months later, the SAS and local soldiers caught the pirates who had attacked the *Fort Colonte*, and killed them during fighting.

There are pirates of a sort operating off the Welsh coast, even these days. They don't attack ships, but many an expensive pleasure boat has been stolen from its berths along the coast.

Bibliography

Breverton, Terry (2003) *The Book of Welsh Pirates and Buccaneers*, Wales Books Glyndwr Publishing

Carse, Robert (1859) *The Age of Piracy*, Robert Hale

Downie, Robert (unknown) *Who's Who in Davy Jones' Locker*, Southgate Books

Gosse, Philip (1924) *The Pirate's Who's Who*, Burt Franklin

Gosse, Philip (1932) *The History of Piracy*, Cassell,

Johnson, Captain Charles (1724 & 1998) *A General History of the Pyrates*

Roberts, W Adolphe (1933) *Sir Henry Morgan*, Hamish Mailton

Rowland, William (1964) *Tomos Prys o Blas Iolyn*, Gwasg Prifysgol Cymru

Richards, Stanley (1966) *Black Bart*, Christopher Davies

Pope, Dudley (1977) *Harry Morgan's Way*, House of Stratus

The *It's Wales* series is just one
of a whole range of Welsh-interest
publications from Y Lolfa. For a full list
of books currently in print, send now
for your free copy of our new, full colour
catalogue. Or simply surf into our website

www.ylolfa.com

for secure on-line ordering.

TALYBONT CEREDIGION CYMRU SY24 5AP
e-bost ylolfa@ylolfa.com
gwefan www.ylolfa.com
ffôn (01970) 832 304
ffacs 832 782